BENEDICT XVI'S REFORM
The Liturgy between Innovation and Tradition

NICOLA BUX

BENEDICT XVI'S REFORM

The Liturgy between
Innovation and Tradition

Preface by Vittorio Messori

Translated by Joseph Trabbic

IGNATIUS PRESS   SAN FRANCISCO

Original Italian edition:
La riforma di Benedetto XVI
© 2008 by Edizioni Piemme Spa, Via Tiziano 32, 20145 Milan, Italy

Front cover photograph:
Pope Benedict XVI
© Stefano Spaziani

Cover designed by Roxanne Mei Lum

TO THE DEAR MEMORY
OF FATHER ADRIANO GARUTI, O.F.M.

CONTENTS

PREFACE

The "liturgical crisis" that followed the Second Vatican Council caused a schism, with many excommunications *latae sententiae*; it provoked unease, polemics, suspicions, and reciprocal accusations. And perhaps it was one of the factors—one, I say, not the only—that brought about the hemorrhaging of practicing faithful, even of those who attended Mass only on the major feasts. Well, it might seem strange, but such a tempest has not diminished but, rather, increased my confidence in the Church.

I will try to explain what I mean, speaking in the first person, returning thus to a personal experience. Some would regard this approach as immodest, but others would see it as the simplest way of being clear and to the point. It happens to be the case that despite my age I have only a very slight recollection of the "old" form of the Church's worship. I grew up in an agnostic household and was educated in secular schools; I discovered the gospel—and began furtively to enter churches as a believer and no longer as a mere tourist—just before the liturgical reform went into force, which for me meant only "the Mass in Italian".

In sum, I caught the tail-end of history. Only a few months later, I would find the altars reversed and some new kitschy piece of junk made of aluminum or plastic brought in to replace the "triumphalism" of the old altars, often signed by masters, adorned with gold and precious marble. But already for some time I had seen—with surprise, in my neophyte innocence—guitars in the place of organs, the jeans of the assistant pastor showing underneath robes that were intended to give the appearance of "poverty", "social" preaching, perhaps with some discussion, the abolition of what they called "devotional accretions", such as making the Sign of the Cross with holy water, kneelers, candles, incense. I even witnessed the occasional disappearance of statues of popular saints; the confessionals, too, were removed, and some, as became the fashion, were transformed into liquor cabinets in designer houses.

Everything was done by clerics, who were incessantly talking about "democracy in the Church", affirming that this was reclaimed by a "People of God", whom no one, however, had bothered to consult. The people, you know, are sovereign; they must be respected, indeed, venerated, but only if they accept the views that are dictated by the political, social, or even religious ruling class. If they do not agree with those who have the power to determine the line to be taken, they must be reeducated according to the vision of the triumphant ideology of the moment. For me, who had just knocked at the door of the Church, gladly welcoming *stabilitas*—which is so attractive and consoling to those who have known only the world's precariousness— that destruction of a patrimony of millennia took me by surprise and seemed to me more anachronistic than modern. It seemed to me that the priests were harming their own people, who, as far as I knew, had not asked for any of this, had not organized into committees for reform, had not signed petitions or blocked streets or railways to bring an end to Latin (a "classist language", but only according to the intellectual demagogues) or to have the priest facing them the whole Mass or to have political chit-chat during the liturgy or to condemn pious practices as alienating, which instead were precious inasmuch as they were a bond with the older generation. There was a revolt on the part of certain groups of faithful—who were immediately silenced, however, and treated by the Catholic media as incorrigibly nostalgic, perhaps a little fascist—united under the motto that came from France: *on nous change la réligion*, "they are changing our religion." In other words, although it was pushed by the champions of "democracy", the liturgical reform (here I am abstracting from the content and am speaking only of the method) was not at all "democratic". The faithful at that time were not consulted, and the faithful of the past were rejected. Is tradition not perhaps, as has been said, the "democracy of the dead"? Is tradition not letting our brothers who have preceded us speak?

Before judging its merits, let me repeat, it must be said that this reform came down from the clergy; the decision was handed down to the "People of God" from above, being thought out, realized, and imposed on those who had not asked for it or who had accepted it only reluctantly. There were some among the disoriented faithful who "voted with their feet", that is to say, they decided to do other things on Sunday rather than attend a liturgy they felt was no longer theirs.

But, as a novice in Catholic matters, there was another reason for my stupor. Not having had particular religious interests "previously", and being a stranger to the life of the Church, I knew that the Second Vatican Council was in progress from some newspaper headlines but did not bother to read the articles. So I knew nothing about the work and the long debates, with clashes between opposing schools, that led to *Sacrosanctum concilium*, the Constitution on the Liturgy, which was, among other things, the first document produced by those deliberations. Along with the other conciliar acts, I read the text "afterward", when faith had suddenly irrupted into my life. I read it, and, as I said, I was left surprised: the revolution I saw in ecclesial practice did not seem to have much to do with the prudent reformism recommended by the Council fathers. I read such things as: "Particular law remaining in force, the use of the Latin language is to be preserved in the Latin rites"; I found no recommendation to reverse the orientation of the altar; there was nothing to justify the iconoclasm of certain clergy—which was a boon for the antique shops—who sold off everything so as to make the churches as bare and unadorned as garages. It was the space for the participating assembly, for encounter and discussion, not for alienating worship or—horror of horrors!—for an insult to the misery of the proletariat with its shining gold and art exhibits.

In short, I could not put the contrasts together: the fanatics of the ecclesial democracy were undemocratic: imposing their own ideas on the "People of God" without concern for what the "People" thought, isolating and ridiculing the dissidents. And the fanatics of "fidelity to the Council"— and they were almost always the same people—did not do what the Council said to do or even did what it recommended not to do.

Decades have passed since then, and what has taken place in the meantime is well known by those who follow the life of the Church. Well, what troubled many often saddened me, too, but it did not, as I said at the beginning, touch my confidence in the Church. It has not touched that confidence because the abuses, the misunderstandings, the exaggerations, the pastoral mistakes were those, as is always the case, of the sons of the Church, not of the Church herself. Thus, if we consider the authentic Magisterium, even in the dark years of chaos and confusion, it never substantially strayed from the guiding principle of *et-et*: renewal and tradition, innovation and continuity, attention to history and awareness of the Eternal, understanding the rite and the mystery of the Sacred, communal sense and attention to the individual, inculturation and catholicity. And, in regard to the summit, the Eucharist: certainly it is a fraternal meal; but just as certainly, it is the spiritual renewal of Christ's sacrifice.

The conciliar document on the liturgy—the real one, not the mythical one—is an exhortation to reform (*Ecclesia semper reformanda*), but there is no revolutionary tone in it, insofar as it finds its inspiration in the considered and, at the same time, open teaching of that great pope who was Pius XII. After Scripture, Pius XII is the most cited source (more than two hundred references) of Vatican II, which, according to the black legend, intended to oppose the very Church he represented. In the many official documents that followed the Council, there is sometimes a pastoral imprudence, especially in an excess of trust in a clergy who took advantage of it, but there is no concession on principles: the abuses were often tolerated in practice but condemned—and it is this that counts in the end—at the magisterial level. Variations in doctrine were not responsible for the worst of what was done but, rather, "indults" that were exploited. It is because of such considerations—for what it is worth—that I and many others were not demoralized even in the most turbulent moments and years: a confidence prevailed that the pastoral misjudgments of which I spoke would be corrected, that the ecclesial antibodies would, as always, react, that the "Petrine principle" would prevail in the end.

It was, in other words, a confidence that times would come like those described—with obligatory realism but also with great hope—by Father Nicola Bux in this book. The recent past has been what it has been; the damage has been massive; some of the rearguard of the old ideologies of "progressivism" still boldly proclaim their slogans; but nothing is lost, because the principles are very clear; they have not been scratched. The problem is certainly not the Council but, if anything, its deformation: the way out of the crisis is in returning to the letter, and to the spirit, of its documents. The author of the pages that follow reminds us that there is work to be done to help many minds that— perhaps without even knowing it—have been led astray. We must help them recover what the Germans call *die katholische Weltanschauung*, the Catholic world view. It is not by chance that I use the German, as everyone knows where that Shepherd comes from who did not expect that ascension to the papacy to be woven into his story as a *patient* and "humble worker in the vineyard of the Lord". If I put the reference to patience in italics, it is because it is one of the interpretive keys to the magisterium of Benedict XVI, as this book will also underscore.

These are pages that Don Nicola Bux was well equipped to write and for which we should be grateful to him. He is a professor of theology and liturgy with important teaching positions, and he has a special knowledge of the liturgy of the Christian East. It is precisely this, among other things, that permits him to show yet another contradiction of the extreme innovators: "Comparative studies show that the Roman liturgy in its preconciliar form was much closer to the Eastern liturgy than its current form." In sum, certain fanatical apostles of ecumenism have, in fact, made the problem of encounter and dialogue worse, distancing themselves from those ancient and glorious Greek, Slav, Armenian, Copt, and other Eastern Churches, in trying to please the members of the official Protestant tradition. The latter, five centuries after the Reformation, seems near to extinction and often is represented only by some theologian with almost no popular following. In some cases, finds itself on the shores of agnosticism and atheism or on those of pentecostals and charismatics belonging to the infinity of groups and sects where everyone invents his rites according to current tastes in a chaos that it would be completely inappropriate to call liturgical.

The plan of the author of these pages is guided by the desire to explain—confuting misunderstandings and errors—the motivations and the content of the *motu proprio Summorum pontificum* through which Pope Benedict, while conserving a single rite for the celebration of the Mass, has permitted two forms of that rite: the ordinary form—the one that came out of the liturgical reform—and the extraordinary form, according to the 1962 Missal of Blessed John XXIII. To give shape to his plan, Don Bux was able to draw, not only on his formation as a scholar, but also on the knowledge of the problems, people, and schools that he acquired in his experience working on commissions and in offices of the Roman Curia. So he has firsthand experience and is not just a specialist and a professor. Nevertheless, he understands that it is not possible to deal with the controversial question about the "return to the Latin Mass" (we put it this way to simplify) without taking account of the theological and liturgical perspective of Joseph Ratzinger and, then, the question of Christian and Catholic worship in general. That is the origin of this book—small and dense—which unites history and the present, theology and current events, and can help those who "already know" about these things to go into them more deeply and reflectively; and it can help the layman who "does not know" to understand the importance, the development, the beauty of this mysterious object that is, for him, the liturgy, which also, even if he is not practicing, involves him or those close to him at important moments in life.

As he himself says, with respectful and affectionate solidarity, the theological and pastoral perspective of Don Bux is the same as that of Joseph Ratzinger, whom he looks upon today as a master, also in respect to two indispensable Christian virtues: patience, as we have already pointed out, and prudence. It is a prudence in which there is a place for renewal, but never forgetting the tradition, for which change does not interrupt continuity. *Ecclesia non facit saltus*: Vatican II is heard and applied as it merits to be, but in its true intention, that of *aggiornamento* and of deepening, without discontinuity with the whole history of Catholic doctrine. These pages also help us to recover that sacred reality expressed by the liturgy: in liturgical action, understanding, in the Enlightenment sense, is not enough; thus, the translations into the vernacular are not enough: it is necessary to rediscover that the liturgy is, first of all, the place of encounter with the living God.

Father Bux, who knows the "world" well, reminds us that there is a mentality that needs to be changed. He thinks that the conditions for this are present: today it is often the young people who find, with awe that becomes passion, the riches with which the Church's treasure chest is full. It is these young people who crowded around the Polish Pope, the great charismatic, and who now crowd around this Bavarian Pope, in whom—beneath the courteous and gentle manner—they intuit the wise project of "restoration" that Joseph Ratzinger has always understood in its noble and necessary sense: the restoration of the *Domus Dei* after one of the many tempests of its history. A project that has been meditated on for many years and that Benedict XVI is now carrying out with courage and patience, because in him, as Don Bux notes, "the patience of love" is at work—love for God and for his Church, certainly, but also for postmodern man, to help him rediscover in liturgical worship the encounter with him who has called himself "the Way, the Truth, and the Life".

VITTORIO MESSORI

I

THE *SACRED* AND *DIVINE* LITURGY

The Liturgy: The Place Where God Meets Man

Why concern oneself with the liturgy? What, briefly and plainly, is the liturgy? No one, even if he is an atheist, can escape the liturgy, at least not in Italy. But this is also true for every other country that has a Christian tradition.

This book is not about an internal debate in the clerical world. It is not about an issue that has nothing to do with ordinary life, a niche reserved for priests and the especially pious. Sooner or later everyone finds himself in church for a wedding, a funeral, a baptism; and we all, despite secularization, participate in such things as processions, benedictions, and pilgrimages.[1]

Thus, when we see the priest kneel or genuflect—something that is becoming increasingly rare—we might be led to think that he does this because he is turning to someone we cannot see. And, consequently, we might happen to ask ourselves if this reality is something that is in front of us, that we see with our eyes, or whether it is something

---

[1] In Italy, religious events, such as Corpus Christi processions, are often important civic events as well.—TRANS.

else. How many times do we ask ourselves at some event: What does it mean? What is behind it?

Saint Paul, for his part, had no doubts: for him, the ritual purity of foods, the feasts and fasts, the calendars are "only a shadow of what is to come; but the substance belongs to Christ" (Col 2:16). Had he, therefore, broken with the widespread opinion among the Jews and the Greeks that no one could see God and live? Had he found a way around the obstacles so that the eye and the ear could endure a vision of the other world? Had he sublimated, as one says today, the need for the sacred or for a transcendent addressee of prayer?

To understand anything, one needs to participate in its nature. The nature of the *sacred* liturgy is to be the time and the place in which God certainly meets man. The method of entering into relationship with him is to render him worship: he speaks to us, and we respond; we give him thanks, and he communicates with us. The sacred liturgy, divine worship, is the sacrifice of what is most dear to us, Jesus Christ and ourselves: thus God, in Jesus, renews the covenant that saves us.

When the Bible says that God has a *name*, it means that he is a person with whom it is possible to enter into a relationship, a being with whom it is possible to have an experience that goes well beyond the everyday. And this is because he, precisely as a person, can manifest himself and communicate himself. For man, this is the first meaning of religion: to bind himself in relationship with God. And, even though it is not possible to know everything about God, he has not drawn near and become concrete in any other religion as he has in Christianity. The Son of God, Jesus Christ, has in large part removed the veil; he has revealed that God is *one* in three persons, similar to *one* people composed of many persons.

In this way, his mystery is still deeper but not more obscure, because, in reality, he has revealed himself as reason, meaning, and word, or, as the three sacred languages say, *Dabar, Lógos, Verbum*. This idea is fundamental and central because it indicates that the person of God is the meaning of the world and that his love is the reason for the world. Because of this, religion is man's supreme act, the *pietas* with which he "offers God splendid praise".

Saint Irenaeus says: "It is not possible to live apart from life, and the means of life is found in fellowship with God; but fellowship with God is to know God, and to enjoy His goodness." So that man might come to understand all this, God began to speak to him, until he revealed himself as the Father who sends the Son (Jn 1:18). Who, nevertheless, "[preserved] the invisibility of the Father, lest man should at any time become a despiser of God, and that he should always possess something towards which he might advance; but, on the other hand, revealing God to men through many dispensations, lest man, falling away from God altogether, should cease to exist. For the glory of God is a living man; and the life of man consists in beholding God."[2] Liturgy is just this, a dispensation, or providential intervention, that is, God's coming among us, providential because it continually heals us and saves us. This is why it is "sacred".

To understand all this, we invite the curious non-believers and "adult" Catholics, the seekers of truth and

---

[2] Irenaeus of Lyons, *Adversus Haereses* 4, 20, 5–7; *Sources chrétiennes* 100:640, 646–48; trans. W. H. Rambaut, in *Irenaeus against Heresies*, in vol. 1 of *Ante-Nicene Fathers*, ed. Alexander Roberts and James Donaldson, rev. A. Cleveland Coxe (1885; Peabody, Mass.: Hendrickson Publishers, 1995), 1:490.

the simple faithful, the emotive liturgists and the rational ones, humbly to let themselves be guided by Benedict XVI, who, as a theologian and peritus at the Council, as the Cardinal Prefect of the Congregation for the Doctrine of the Faith, and now as Bishop of Rome, knows a great deal about the liturgy.

The Liturgy: "Heaven on Earth"

Cosmic praise, which "goes from the Seraphim to the Angels and Archangels, to man and to all the creatures which, together, reflect God's beauty and are praise of God", is the essential characteristic of a mysterious theologian of the sixth century who hid himself under the pseudonym of Dionysius the Areopagite (for this reason he is also called Pseudo-Dionysius), who derived his name from one of those among the listeners who opened themselves to the faith after Saint Paul's celebrated sermon at the Areopagus (Acts 17:16–33). Benedict XVI spoke of him in a Wednesday general audience on May 14, 2008, further noting that

> since the creature is praise of God, Pseudo-Dionysius' theology became a liturgical theology: God is found above all in praising him, not only in reflection; and the liturgy is not something made by us, something invented in order to have a religious experience for a certain period of time; it is singing with the choir of creatures and entering into cosmic reality itself. And in this very way the liturgy, apparently only ecclesiastical, becomes expansive and great; it becomes our union with the language of all creatures.[3]

---

[3] Benedict XVI, *Church Fathers and Teachers from Saint Leo the Great to Peter Lombard* (San Francisco: Ignatius Press, 2010), p. 28.

This vision of the liturgy, which, as scholars know, is not only that of the Byzantine East but is also at the root of the Latin liturgies, such as the Roman and the Ambrosian liturgies, begs to be rediscovered. Instead of getting caught up in mutual censures, a comparison is in order between those who see liturgy "from below", so to speak, and those who admire it above all "from above".

But there is more: Dionysius' cosmic and liturgical theology is also mystical and is, therefore, personal and sacramental. God alone knows how much need there is to recover this aspect after the emphasis that has been placed on the communitarian dimension in the last several decades. People ask more and more for respect for a personal space of silence, of intimate participation of faith in the sacred mysteries and in the public and solemn prayer of the Church, as was reiterated from Pius X to Pius XII. So, to give an example, can one ignore the fact that the rituals envision the celebration of baptism for only one child, similar to the way in which the funeral rite is envisioned for only one person? Why should it not be possible for only one person to receive Communion just as confession is envisioned for only one person? Why must everything be reduced to the communitarian aspect? In the Gospel, Jesus also encountered many people individually, and, right up to the present day, he gives himself to each person in a personal way.

Thus, the Pope always underscores the passage in Pseudo-Dionysius from the mystic understood as equivalent to the sacramental to the mystic understood as the personal and intimate expression of "the journey of the soul to God". The liturgy must, in fact, stimulate the search for God, the encounter with him, and conversion to him. It invites us to turn to the Lord, turning our gaze away from ourselves or other creatures, even the celebrating priest. It is the priest himself who asks this with the *Sursum corda*, as we answer him with the *Habemus ad Dominum*. Dionysius' liturgy, then, is nothing other than the manifestation of the sacred reality of God.

It is said that life is sacred. One stands in silence before the sacrality of death. Still further, one finds oneself reflecting on the fact that good and evil play in our mind in relation to what we know of the sacred, in relation to the idea we have of the mysterious, fascinating, and frightening, and, at the same time, alluring and terrible. What human being does not feel such a mystery playing out inside him in his experience of life? The sacred is precisely this region in which the possible responses can only be moral. And this is the case only if it is founded in a God who is wholly other with respect to man.

If on so many sides one invokes an ethical code that regulates our relationships with each other, this means that without knowing it we are seeking the foundation of human existence. Nevertheless, if we find ourselves confronted with the current moral problems that we do, is it not because, separating man from God—indeed, for some theologians, it is a separating of Christ from God—God is made distant from man? Thus, while, on one hand, ethics is rejected so that each person decides for himself what he wants, on the other hand, ethics is invoked because it is believed that it can fix man, make him just, and, finally, in this way resolve social conflicts.

But in combining the problem of faith with the problem of ethics, it is first of all necessary that we ask ourselves about what we think is important, what is worship, or *cult* (in Latin, *colere*), what is the *liturgy* (a Greek term that in classical antiquity meant public service but came to mean worship of God)—worship and liturgy, in which, as we said, we invest our time. Worship and liturgy are important because it is here, in the liturgies of Baptism and Easter, of the Eucharist and death, that man touches the sacred. The liturgy is sacred because it comes down from above, from God who is in heaven; this is why it is "heaven on earth". The Eastern Christians and great popes such as Gregory and Leo say that the liturgy is divine, but so do the councils of Trent and Vatican II. One of the constitutions of the latter council has the title *On the Sacred Liturgy*: the liturgy, then, is sacred because it expresses the sacred and because the sacred breathes in the liturgy. This means that through the liturgy one is in the presence of God, the *shekinah*, the Jews say. It is commonly said that it is *sacrosanct*: it is the new and definitive life of Christ—eschatology, a mysterious Greek term— that has irrupted into time and the cosmos.

The liturgy is sacred because it is not made by the hands of man; were it otherwise, it would be idolatry. In the liturgy is the burning bush that is not consumed, the heavenly Jerusalem that comes down from heaven, the Incarnation and birth of Jesus, the Transfiguration and Calvary, the Resurrection and Pentecost. In a word, the ecstasy of beauty that pours the fire of God into the hearts of men.

So we understand that the liturgy is the place where heaven and earth touch. Thus, the Pope's catechesis on Dionysius of which we spoke earlier helps us to understand the sacred better, that is, the mystery that makes itself present and brings about the moral elevation of man. We also understand that the sacred is the fundamental law of the liturgy because it comes down from the presence of God. Consequently, disobeying the norms that recall the liturgy's sacredness, in the name of the will to create it from our own resources, is to desacralize and secularize the liturgy.

Rediscovering the Courage for the Sacred

Whether it be the ancient civil liturgies or the liturgy of the modern rock concert, both celebrate idols, "the work of men's hands" (Ps 115:4). But in recent times, even religious liturgies—the word "liturgy" is preferred over "worship" today, perhaps because it emphasizes the role of the people in the sacred action more than the time given to God—as we said, have become a "dance around the golden calf" [4] that we ourselves are. This was noted, with sadness, by Ratzinger, when he was still a cardinal, in a shocking meditation for the Via Crucis in 2005, in which he frankly but effectively pointed out what the liturgy is not. This is what the liturgy becomes because of the simple fact that we are not God and are off track if we worship ourselves.

If we have arrived at this point, it is because the liturgical movement has suffered deformation, whether from those who think what is new is always better or from those who think that returning to the ancient is always the best thing to do in every circumstance. We shall see just how wrongheaded and contradictory this is.

Approached in this way, the liturgy was no longer something received from above, as at Sinai the divine word, which is the law by which we walk, was received. It has become, rather, just the fashioning from below of the golden calf around which we dance. Thus divine worship is no longer my expecting everything from the Lord but, rather, what I myself have decided to expect. How much responsibility the bishops and priests have for what has happened! In practice, it means giving in to the temptation of taking God's place.

[4] J. Ratzinger, *The Spirit of the Liturgy*, trans. John Saward (San Francisco: Ignatius Press, 2000), p. 23.

The liturgy, let us be clear, is always in need of reform, because worship must always return to the sacred, that is, to the relationship with the transcendent God who has become incarnate. But the liturgy comes down from heaven to the earth; it can never be "do-it-yourself liturgy". This is also true because if the liturgy were not sacred, if worship were not divine, it would be of no use except to represent ourselves, and, above all, it would not save man and the world; it would not make man holy.

But there is another important aspect that pertains to the liturgy. It is something that is always mentioned by Pseudo Dionysius, one of the exponents of "negative theology", which reminds us that the liturgy cannot say and explain everything. And this is because one cannot know everything about God but only that which Jesus Christ has revealed and the Church proposes for belief.

This is why the liturgy, too, like theology, is *apophatic*: "It is easier for us to say what God is not rather than to say what he truly is", the Pope says in the catechesis on Pseudo-Dionysius, adding further that,

> although Dionysius shows us, following Proclus, the harmony of the heavenly choirs in such a way that it seems that they all depend on one another, it is true that on our journey toward God we are still very far from him. Pseudo-Dionysius shows that in the end the journey to God is God himself, who makes himself close to us in Jesus Christ. Thus, a great and mysterious theology also becomes very concrete, both in the interpretation of the liturgy and in the discourse on Jesus Christ.[5]

[5] Benedict XVI, *Church Fathers*, p. 29.

With the coming of Jesus, in fact, the profane has not completely disappeared; still it is continuously pressed by the sacred, which is dynamic, on the way to fulfillment: "For this reason we must rediscover the courage for the sacred, the courage to distinguish; not in order to fence off but in order to transform, to be truly dynamic." [6]

Signs Evoke and Point to the Mystery

To say that there is the sense of the sacred in the old Mass, the Mass of Pius V, the extraordinary form of the Roman liturgy, also entails asking oneself what makes this so and in what way it manifests itself. One aspect, for example, is the distinction that it establishes between the place of the priest and the place of the faithful, which, nevertheless, is never *distance* or separation. If that in fact were so, what might be said of the iconostases of the Eastern liturgy? This distinction has a precise value; this is why it cannot be abolished in the way it has been in the communitarian Protestant structures.

But there are other ways that the sacred is present and expresses itself in the old Mass. It is in the Sign of the Cross and the genuflections. It is in the silence of the faithful during the Eucharistic Prayer, which is not shouted but spoken *submissa voce* [7] to signify even our voice's submission and humility before God. Furthermore, it is in the sacred language, with its contemporary incomprehensibility: our Latin, but also the old Greek and the Church Slavonic of

[6] J. Ratzinger, *Ministers of Your Joy*, trans. R. Nowell (Ann Arbor, Mich.: Redeemer Books, 1989), p. 123.

[7] Council of Trent, can. 9; Denzinger-Schönmetzer, *Enchiridion Symbolorum*, no. 1759.

the Byzantines. In this connection, we must try to understand why it is not the purpose of the vernacular to render the liturgy completely comprehensible. This is so true that, even when the vernacular is used, it does not lessen the concern to provide introductions and mystagogy.

The sacred, therefore, is in the instruments and the signs that evoke the mystery. This is also true for the much celebrated signs of the postconciliar Mass. Nonetheless, the mystery is never completely identical with the signs. What use would they be if they did not point to something else? Moreover, the signs of the liturgy are *sacred* and *holy* because they contain what they signify—definitive salvation from sin, new life in Jesus Christ—and are efficacious for those who receive them; that is why they are *sacra*ments. Thus, as Saint Augustine teaches, the difference between sacred signs and natural, conventional, and symbolic signs remains.

With the sacraments, above all with the Blessed Sacrament, the sacred goes out from itself to consecrate the world. The Israelites who went up to the Temple to worship separated themselves from the rest of the world by means of the Court of Women and the Court of Pagans. But Jesus, tearing down the barriers between God and man and among men themselves, wanted to bring God's truth—which is the sacred—out of the Temple, the *fanum* of the ancients. Of course, shoes are still removed and heads are still covered, but it has become evident that all of that has a point only if one receives a new *heart* and makes *it* the Temple. This is what is meant when it is said that true worshippers worship the Father in spirit and in truth.

They will continue to build temples and pray inside and outside of them, but, above all, they will pray by entering into their room, that is, their heart, where God sees in secret. The Catholic liturgy leads to all this. The old Mass, thus, represents a powerful means of recovering balance after the liturgical deformations we have witnessed.

Whether one understands everything or only part of what happens in the funeral or nuptial liturgy, the mystery is still there and draws you in. . . . This is faith in the supernatural mystery, present before me here and now: I *believe* that you are here present, and I *dedicate* myself to you, and I express this through ritual forms and practices. In this sense, the Christian faith fulfills man's religious sense.

All of this demands a continual *conversion*, a beholding of his Countenance before me. Sinking to his knees becomes the creature's most eloquent expression in the face of the mystery that is present. This is the center of worship: I am aware that you are here, and I give you importance. Truly, as Joseph Ratzinger notes in *Introduction to Christianity*: "[F]aith is located in the act of conversion, in the turn of one's being from the worship of the visible and practicable to trust in the invisible." [8]

The Importance of Tradition

The liturgy has the capacity to bind us, in the present, to the structures of the past as a permanent value, to immerse us in what we call *tradition*. But we live in a time that wants to replace tradition with innovation.

This tendency threatens the essential issue of faith, that is, the difference between the visible and the invisible, which Judaeo–Christian revelation mitigated from the moment the

[8] J. Ratzinger, *Introduction to Christianity*, trans. J. R. Foster and M. J. Miller, rev. ed. (San Francisco: Ignatius Press, 2004), p. 88.

Eternal entered into the world: "No one has ever seen God; the only-begotten Son, who is in the bosom of the Father, he has made him known" (Jn 1:18). Jesus did this once for all; he showed us and he shows us God; he explains him by taking up a piece of bread and a chalice. This is the gesture that makes us see with our eyes, touch with our hands (cf. 1 Jn 1:1–3) him whom no one has ever seen.

But the very moment this revelation approaches our human measure in the liturgy, it hides itself. This is just what occurred in the Incarnation and in the Passion, when God made himself so small and near as to be imperceptible, to be killed, and to lose the appearance of his equality with God.

But at this point the initial question is asked again: What is *reality*? Is historical *fact* the only thing that is real, as Kant and Vico hold? Marx says that this claim is insufficient. For him, only what *can be done* and transformed is real. Thus, it was no longer enough to turn to the Eternal, as in the Middle Ages, or to the past, as in the brief period of historicism. It has thus been maintained that one must project oneself into the future, for which an "anthropological turn" is necessary. How much Rahner, who used this expression, has influenced the postconciliar liturgy is easy to verify. If man is recreated and manipulated, this can, *a fortiori*, likewise be done with the liturgy as well as with the faith and dogma. From this perspective, they are no longer a fact but something made, no longer tradition but progress.

It is not that the faith and the liturgy should avoid development. But should such development be carried to the point of turning their nature and structure upside down, turning them toward man rather than God? Did not the revelation of Jesus Christ resolve this apparent conflict, and did it not convey the liturgy as the word of God addressed to us men and as a solemn prayer addressed to God the Father? Eastern and Western Christians saw the priest turned toward God at the altar and only occasionally turned toward the people for greetings and exhortations. Then the West, in the last forty years, took another path with the permanent turning of the priest toward the people.

But along with worship that has lost its proper orientation, the faith, too, has gotten off track, has lost the *amen*—which in Hebrew has the same root as *faith*—that meant standing firm in the faith, remaining united with God. To say *amen* to him in whom I believe is to recognize in him the meaning of reality, indeed, reason itself, the *Logos*, the word, the truth. Saint Paul reassures: "I know whom I have believed" (2 Tim 1:12). This is why in the liturgy "amen" is used to translate the expressions "it is so" (*così è*) and "so be it" (*così sia*).

It is from this rational root that *rational* worship blossoms forth. Man's stability is possible only if he makes truth his foundation: this is why the act of faith is convinced adherence to the *Logos* who is truth. "Believe also in me" (Jn 14:1), Jesus says. Meaning, foundation, and truth, inseparably, make the *mystery* comprehensible. This word "mystery" has been misappropriated today and used to submerge into an ahistorical indeterminacy the figure and work of Jesus Christ and the worship owed to God the Father through him. It is used, furthermore, to multiply signs and symbols designed to make people dream of the feeling rather than to make faith possible as an understanding of truth.

Rightly understood, mystery includes us; it continually precedes and transcends us. We cannot grasp the mystery but only be grasped by it. This is why the liturgy is not something made by us. This was the understanding of mystery postulated by the Fathers: liturgy as a personal adherence to the person of

Jesus, an *encounter* with him, to touch him with my hands as the Apostle Thomas did. He is God, who has drawn near, who is present in the world.

Without his presence, there is no liturgy. This is the reason why it is essential to emphasize the tabernacle. It is the tent that the Word has pitched among us out of love, the meaning of the cosmos and of history. Because of his love for us, his love for me, I am able to speak to him in intimate terms.[9]

In the love between a man and a woman, the meaning of existence is a "you" (*tu*), who knows me and loves me. It is similar in our relation to God, who is a "you" who is intangible and without equal. But the encounter with this "you" is never taken for granted, because doubt and darkness threaten it. It is the vigil, the expectation, of love, like the vigils of a bride, which fills and forms the liturgy, beginning with the Easter Vigil, the mother of all vigils. "I believe in you, Jesus of Nazareth, as the meaning (*logos*) of the world and of my life." [10] The "I" and the "you" intersect, inserting man into the "we" of the community of believers.

The Liturgy as Rule of Faith

The liturgy asks us to entrust ourselves to the Word, who is generated but *non factum*—and never made by man—precisely to make what we do possible. If faith belongs to

---

[9] Bux says: "... che posso dirgli *tu*." Literally: "... that I am able to say 'you' to him." Modern English lacks the distinction that Italian makes between a formal word for "you" (*lei*) and an informal one (*tu*). In proper Italian, *tu* is used only for those with whom one is close. Bux's point is that God's deep love for us makes it appropriate for us to address him informally as *tu*.—Trans.

[10] Ratzinger, *Introduction to Christianity*, p. 81.

the realm of our fundamental decisions, it is expressed continuously through the one form of the liturgy, which, not
by chance, is composed of the signs of what is most basic
to man's life: bread, water, wine, oil, . . . word, love. It is
the divine reality that consecrates the human reality.

Thus the liturgy is the form that gathers up all of reality
and its meaning *in a stable way*, a reality and a meaning that
we do not create because then it would no longer be precisely that, reality and meaning, that is, what is given and
what is a fact: "I received from the Lord what I also deliv-
ered to you" (1 Cor 11:23), Paul says. The liturgy, then, is
received from tradition: it is a gift that is received. And it is
itself tradition. To believe is to trust; this is why we respond
to the *Logos*, who makes all things exist, recognizing that
the invisible is *more real* than the visible. All of this is in
contrast to the positivism that acknowledges only what is
apparent, the phenomenal. This positivism also causes the
liturgy to be tempted by appearance and the spectacular.
Whoever sets tradition in opposition to innovation forgets
that the word "tradition" comes from a word that implies
change and life. The liturgy, like the Church, is living
tradition.

But if the Eucharist is a mystery that is present to be believed,
that is, to be received as a gift, to understand it one must
begin with the fact that God gave his Son, Jesus. It is, therefore, the mystery of the presence of God come to earth in
our flesh that we recognize and call sacrament, that is, sacred
and objective reality, a gift of his love. This is why the work
of God is to believe in him whom God has sent (cf. Jn 6:29).

This mystery is not an *enigma*, but a reality that is quite
rational: it is that which bursts forth when man encounters
Christ. This is the beauty of the liturgy of the Church, of

the prayer that, as Saint Augustine observes, renders the
heart capable of hoping in God.[11] With the coming of Christ,
something new entered into human worship, that is, in the
important relation that man has always sought with God:
the symbols, the objects, the figures can no longer announce
something that is to come but only a truth that is present
thanks to the Incarnation.[12] Thus the history of the liturgy
describes the Church who receives this gift and, with the
guidance of the Spirit, develops it in sacramental form. For
this reason, remembering him means, not only repeating
the liturgy, but receiving him as a gift and entering into
him. The words of Jesus Christ are spirit and life, and so
the Spirit does everything together with him when he is
invoked. He does this at the moment the priest says: "Take
and eat" and afterward, too.[13] Christ always comes *first* and,
with him, the universal Church.

Just as faith comes through hearing (cf. Rom 10:17), so also
does the liturgy. It is not a philosophy, which comes through
reflection: no, before my thought, there is the word of God.
Just as faith comes to man from beyond him, so also does
the liturgy, the responsible reception of the unthinkable.
Because of this, the word of the liturgy is not at my disposal or interchangeable; rather, it always precedes my
thought, just as God is always *before* me.

If thought is an interior fact, something that is mine, the
word and the liturgy have a social character and finality: they
are that which unites. At this point it is clear that, like faith,
the liturgy has a dialogical structure, so that as it delineates

[11] Benedict XVI, Encyclical *Spe salvi* (November 30, 2007), no. 33.
[12] Cf. Benedict XVI, Post-synodal Apostolic Exhortation *Sacramentum car-itatis* (February 22, 2007), no. 11.
[13] Ibid., no. 13.

the image of man, the image of God appears: an interweaving of relations that permits man to enter into relationship with God and his brothers. How important it is that in divine worship sight, hearing, touch, taste, smell all have their respective role! Will we not help man's gaze to see the image of God in Christ? And his hearing to receive the word? "God wishes to approach man only through man; he seeks out man in no other way but in his fellow humanity." [14]

Along the lines of what Plato says of man in the *Symposium* (191d), we must recall once more the *symbolic* capacity of the liturgy—the symbol of faith, the *Credo*, is an illustrious example—a capacity that is linked to *symbállein*, to bringing the visible and the invisible together to express and facilitate precisely man's unity. The liturgy's structure is dogmatic: as the original meaning of "dogma" is to make possible, the communal profession of faith makes possible the communal worship "of what we know", that is, worship in spirit and truth. The liturgy is a *rule of faith* because it regulates the language of the faith that is synthesized in dogmas. Thus we see that the opposition between the Fathers and the Scholastics, suggested by some, does not hold.

So, in the *Credo* we rediscover the form of the liturgy—I believe/*amen*—which is also the form of our conversion, which is recalled in the priest's exhortation: "Let us lift up our hearts", and its response: "We lift them up to the Lord." The prayer of the liturgy is directed to God, and this is simultaneously our unified giving of *glory* to him. We are united in heart and spirit. As a spiritual reality, the Church manifests herself in the liturgy, which cannot be mere organization. The liturgy understands itself to be completely

---

[14] Ratzinger, *Introduction to Christianity*, p. 94.

relative to God as worship that celebrates him and is his glorification: this is manifested precisely in the direction of the prayer, which is *toward God*, to the East. The Church descends from heaven from the very creation of the world and, proclaiming the truth to men that she is the way to heaven, must bring the redeemed world in herself to heaven. The imperfection of the human liturgy, which, therefore, must continually refer back to God, achieves its purpose. In this sense Christianity reveals its nature as *way*, since it is nothing other than the person of Christ.

Here we have arrived at understanding what communion is, namely, a reality that is open and oriented toward God because it comes down from God. It is a communion that is born in the gaze of the priest and the faithful toward the Lord and that opens onto eternity. And we also understand why the liturgy depends on believing, the *lex credendi* closely linked to the *lex orandi*. In this fashion the liturgy offers to man the truth as way. The Eastern liturgy defines Christ as the "light of reason" because he teaches the true philosophy. Thus the liturgy makes us philosophers: "Believe, then, that the presence of divinity is there", Saint Ambrose says to neophytes. "You believe in his action but do not believe in his presence? How could there be action if it were not preceded by presence?" [15]

---

[15] Saint Ambrose, *De Mysteriis* III, 8; *Sources chrétiennes* 25 bis: 158.

II

THE ONE TO WHOM WE DRAW NEAR
IN DIVINE WORSHIP

*Looking upon the Crucified Lord Orients Worship
and the Heart*

Often one hears it said that there is no need to pray to God
to ask him for what we need but only or above all to praise
him, for he is not a stopgap for our insufficiencies and inca-
pacities but is completely in tune with our reality and earthly
life.

The liturgy, in fact, contemplates both and perhaps more
possibilities, as the Psalms of the Bible attest: God *gives meaning* to our life and makes it possible for us to receive meaning in our need. Thus, the more man goes out from his "I"
toward God, the more deeply he comes to himself.

This makes us understand that the itinerary of the liturgy
follows that of the faith as it is described by Joseph Ratzinger in *Introduction to Christianity*. Consider this example
of prayer that looks to faith: when Jesus prays to the Father
that his disciples *become* one as he and the Father *are* one,
he expresses humility before the mystery. This helps us to
remain modest, to hold together the *God with us* of the

Old Testament and the "you" (*tu*) addressed to the Father
of the New Testament. At the same time, his gaze turned
to the Father discloses to us what it means for God to be a
Person, making us understand that existence is interrela-
tionship (and this is why it is also at the foundation of the
liturgy). There is such an intimate relation between the Father
and Son that the latter can say, "My teaching is not mine"
(Jn 7:16). This is the paradox that leads in a certain sense
to understanding the mystery in a new way: understanding
who man is depends on an understanding of who God is.
This is why his word joined itself to the flesh.

At this point the second step is taken: *I believe in Jesus
Christ*. He, the union between word and flesh, is the meaning, the aim of life: the liturgy, therefore, must have such
an orientation because it has life.

The Cross, with its four cardinal points, enters to orient
our heart and the gaze of prayer. Faith is connected with
love-Christ, who gives himself. The Word made flesh is
Love, love for the many. "[T]he challenge of love [is] the
challenge of faith ... faith that is not love is not a really
Christian faith." [1] The orientation of faith to love is evident
in what Saint Paul writes in Philippians 2:5–11. In this passage we see that corresponding to Christ's abasement is the
proskynēsis, the profound obeisance of the cosmos: "The cosmic liturgy, the adoring homage of the universe, centers
round this Lamb (Rev 5)." [2]

Can it be any different for our liturgy, given the desire to
accentuate its eschatological dimension? Would we not do
everything we could to imitate this cosmic liturgy and put

[1] J. Ratzinger, *Introduction to Christianity*, trans. J. R. Foster and M. J. Miller,
rev. ed. (San Francisco: Ignatius Press, 2004), p. 209.
    [2] Ibid., p. 221.

all the necessary conditions in place, with or without kneelers? Do not Eastern Christians prostrate themselves without them? We should recall that precisely this witness, which responds to Christ's martyrdom, is the origin of worship and form of the early Church structures known as *martyria*. They, in fact, arose at the sites of crucifixion, of martyrdom and martyr's tombs: where their bodies were buried, there too Christ's body is consecrated, that is, immolated, buried, and resurrected.

In such a way, worship and the temple become a place of resistance to any idolatry of political power. This is, in a certain sense, the true political response of the Church, as the twentieth century—neither more nor less than did the first centuries of persecution—showed us. Here the Church—who expresses herself not only in the power of a visual array of ministers at the altar but in the impotence of the priest who can also celebrate the supreme sacrifice alone—is truly configured and manifested. It is a permanent critique of the world, of that world which penetrates the Church, pressing her to conform to it. Thus, the Cross, at the center of the liturgy, permanently "challenges" the Church and compels her—starting with her leader—to orient herself toward him who is crucified there. Should our physical and interior gaze turn to something other than the Lord? The sacred liturgy is revealed at this point to be a theology of the Cross.

The liturgy calls our Lord Jesus Christ "the only begotten Son of God", "Savior", and "Redeemer". Christ, as man, assumes all of us, making us his body: "[Y]ou are all one in Christ Jesus" (Gal 3:28). He takes up our future and gives us a foretaste of it. He is the new Adam, who came with the Incarnation, was resurrected at Easter, ascended into heaven (and we with him as our head), and sent us his transforming Spirit at Pentecost. He is our Passover, because we all pass through him, who has opened himself to us, having torn down the walls of his existence,[3] as the lance opened up his heart (Jn 19:34). There is no image of Easter/Passover more eloquent than this and, even more important, no deed more efficacious.

Thus, the liturgy cannot be an attraction to anything other than the one who said: "I ... will draw all men to myself" (Jn 12:32). Where else, then, should the cross be fixed than at the center of the highest place, the altar where he is sacrificed? The altar is also the symbol of the sepulcher from which he rose, according to the ancient tradition common to both East and West.

It is from here that the sacraments flow and, therefore, the Church also, as the new communion possible among men. The permanent efficaciousness of the sacraments derives from Christ's *opening up* of himself, that is, from the truth of Easter: like Christ, we too must receive and give back. He has given himself for many, the Roman Canon says, following the account of the institution of the Eucharist (Mk 14:24). It is his being totally open that makes Christ our Redeemer. In looking upon Christ, who is pierced (Jn 19:37), the meaning of our worship is synthesized: in tearing away our gaze from every other being or every other thing of the past or the future, the *today* of the liturgy loves and focuses in the present on him who is hope itself.

Thus, in Christ, the Church already knows the face of him who must come. This is why she must focus herself,

[3] Ibid., p. 240.

orient herself to him, for the future depends on him. In fact, he will return with the Cross. But in the sacred liturgy, he already returns to us at the same moment he goes to the Father (Jn 14:28). In this way, service to men is shown to be inseparable from the glorification of God, as are prayer and fraternity: the symbol is the arms of Christ open wide on the Cross. It is the primal form of the liturgy, of the *orante* according to the Fathers and as depicted in the catacomb paintings.

The eucharistic sacrifice is grafted onto all of this, which makes the Church at the same time not only the place of God's nearness but also the place of his hiddenness. For this reason, "[w]hoever puts himself at God's disposal disappears with him in the cloud, into oblivion and insignificance"— like Mary (Lk 1:35)—"and precisely in this way acquires a share in his glory."[4] At this point we understand better why the Eucharist is at the center of Christian worship and is so in a superabundant way, in the way that Mary's intercession can obtain and anticipate the Lord's *hour* at Cana in Galilee. Only thus is the Church, the house of God, also the house of the people of God.

The Eucharist as Essence of Christian Worship

A new and unheard of event has taken place: "[I]n Christ God was reconciling the world to himself" (2 Cor 5:19); therefore, Catholic worship reconciles man with God. It is the ultimate goal of the expiatory goat, of the satisfaction-reparation owed by man. We see more of the true meaning of the Cross as the center of liturgy: God does not wait but

[4] Ibid., p. 273.

comes to meet the guilty and reconciles them. This is the movement from Incarnation to death.

Unlike Old Testament worship, that of the New Testament, because of the Cross, becomes a movement from above to below, from heaven to earth. It is, as the Fathers say, a philanthropic shift. Thus, the true worship is born, which consists in the grateful reception of God's salvation, that is, thanksgiving, Eucharist, justly understood as the *essential form* of Christian worship. The logic of the Christian sacrifice, then, consists in welcoming God, without whom we can do nothing, and in letting ourselves be completely overtaken by him. Thus, the liturgy is the *opus Dei*, because we permit God to work and act in us. Hence, *opus*, or in Greek, *ergon* (which forms part of the root of the word "liturgy"), is referred to as the *laos* (the other part of the root), the sacred people of God, but with the understanding that the initiative is divine rather than human.

"He suffered under Pontius Pilate, was crucified, died, and was buried": the liturgy and the altar with the cross represent this article of the Creed in plastic form. In this way they also and simultaneously express the justice that man owes to God and the grace that God bestows on man.

The Cross and the liturgy of the New Testament are explained by the Old Testament's theology of worship (one thinks of the Letter to the Hebrews in relation to Psalm 49:9–14) because they are also in a certain sense the ascending movement of man and, with him, the cosmos to God. It is the Yes with which man freely responds to God. This is true worship and true sacrifice because, in reality, everything belongs to God. Man cannot give anything to God in place of himself (his life: Mk 8:37).

Thus, worship is in vain if it points toward things or animals. In this sense, the Letter to the Hebrews shows the failure of religious cults. This is the true meaning of substitution-expiation-reparation-representation. In the Letter to the Hebrews, Jesus Christ, a layman without a special office in the worship of Israel, becomes the one true priest. His death took place outside the gates of the city, in the space of the profane, and, through the offering he made of himself, he became the one liturgy that has transformed the world into a temple. In this way, what was profane becomes sacred.

The orientation toward the Cross, therefore, opens the space of the liturgical action that otherwise was closed, because the blood of Christ is understood as the expression of the love that goes to the very end (Jn 13:1), the total love of the *I am*. This is the redemption, the reconciliation of man and the world. "There is no other kind of worship and no other priest but he who accomplished it: Jesus Christ." [5]

Here the essence of Christian worship takes shape, the Eucharist, which consists in the absolute dedication of love: offering our bodies as a living, holy sacrifice, pleasing to God (cf. Rom 12:1). Our worship is also logical, rational (cf. ibid.), because love is the true logic of life. Divine love has become human, and it is represented by Jesus, who has vouched for us before God. And we let ourselves be seized by him because we cannot justify ourselves, placing our guilt, like Adam, upon others. We must, rather, open up to the gift of Jesus' love for us, a love that justifies us, that unites us with each other and with him, transforming us into true worshippers of God. This is the spirit and the truth of worship, which is therefore *logical*: worshipping the Father as my origin and rediscovering myself as his son.

[5] Ibid., p. 287.

But this does not mean, then, that Christian worship is reduced to fraternal love—which would be fragile—because it is interested in getting something back; rather, it is disinterested because it loves God first of all and gives glory only to him. Worship, first and before all else, can be nothing other than adoration, because this is man's supreme act; it is true and definitive liberation, insofar as it is going out of oneself, that is, sacrifice.

Christian worship, therefore, has as its constitutive principle, going out of self to God and to man. This is the salvation that makes the Cross life "for many" (Mt 26:28). Thus, adoration always coincides with the Cross and pain: from the love that constitutes sacrifice flows suffering, the pain and death of the grain of wheat that in this way is able to bear fruit.

The Cross, which extends to the four cardinal points, expresses such dismemberment and laceration that one must make a similar return to Christ in love. Thus, one cannot get around the Cross, even to enter into dialogue with exponents of other religions or those of no religion, under pain of falling back into the logic of animal sacrifices and the trappings of Hebrew worship. The apostolate and mission flow from the Cross and nowhere else.

But it is the fullness of love and not the sum of pain that redeems the world; indeed, it is love that gives meaning to pain. The Cross completely reveals man because it responds to the exigence of justice, and this is why, as we have said, it will also be present at the Last Judgment. Man, in his presentiment of this, is revealed to himself both in his lack of truth and his aspiration to justice.

But the Cross also completes God's revelation: *regnavit a ligno Deus*. The Cross is the revelation of God, who descends into the human abyss, even into hell, to save man at the same time that he judges him. Thus, the Cross is at the center of revelation and so also of the orientation of prayer and worship insofar as it is the center of and revelation of divine and human love. If the Old Testament says that love is *as* strong as death (Song 8:6), with the New Testament we must say that love is *stronger* than death, thanks to the Resurrection of Jesus: he loved others and so continues to live and exist in another: it is the logic of love at the physical level.

But beyond physical reality there is the reality of the Spirit: the flesh is of no avail, Jesus says (Jn 6:63). Christ's flesh in the sacrament is not corruptible flesh, but the risen body, his Divine Person incarnate; for Paul, body and spirit are one thing and not opposed to each other. Christ the Lord makes all things new (cf. Rev 21:15) in and with the liturgy, which contemplates the new Jerusalem descending from heaven into the midst of men. Thus, we are certain that the world is continually redeemed once for all, and in every generation it is saved, not by the utopias of values—today's legalism and pacifism—but by the new law and by the peace that Christ alone gives in the liturgy and we receive in faith.

Jesus rose, the disciples said. But it is also true that God brought this about out of love so as to give Jesus a greater life. He did not return to the previous *bíos* that was subject to death but received a new life, *zōē*—as the Byzantine liturgy says of baptism—different and definitive, eternal. In the end, the gospel is the announcement that this eternal life has broken into history, and we begin to experience it in the community gathered in the Church, the gathering together, the sacred *sinassi*. It is here we can experience the love that has *passed beyond* death—the Passover—and has inaugurated the new situation of men, that of us Christians.

The first of them is Jesus: that he is alive in a different and new way we understand from the moment his word inflames the hearts of those who hear it and opens the eyes of those who see him break the bread. All of this is worship, the liturgy. Everything we have described happens in it. Indeed, we can say that it is the *mode* in which the risen Lord appears, manifests himself. Thus, the Resurrection and the liturgy constitute a single theology. Thus, he is touched, recognized, drawn near to not only as the Risen One but, still more, as the Living One. This is why the liturgy is a permanent miracle: because of his presence, it continually lifts us up again.

The meaning of Christian worship is, therefore, entirely founded on the event of the Resurrection, as the Gospel accounts of the apparitions of the risen Christ show. What is an apparition if not someone presenting himself in an unexpected way? It occurs outside of us and escapes all our uncertainties. This is why on Easter morning the disciples said: "The Lord is truly risen!" The Lord defeated death and reappeared in all his power. The disciples were dissuaded from seeking in the sepulcher him who was, on the contrary, alive. They had to seek him in their unified gathering, for there he would be revealed. Nothing is impossible to God. Is not all of this reasonable? So, we can believe in the love that has conquered death; we can have faith, and reason, thus, broadens and attains its fulfillment.

But the liturgy still adds something further: the risen Lord is coming; his coming is nigh. The theologians say, in a way that may be hard to grasp, that the eschaton is always imminent from the moment he ascended into heaven, from the moment he can hear us. And this is because with Easter an opening between God and man, between heaven and earth, is produced; indeed, heaven has descended to earth—just as Jacob dreamed and Jesus promised: "[Y]ou will see heaven opened, and the angels of God ascending and descending upon the Son of man" (Jn 1:51; cf. also Gen 28:12). It is a stairway upon which spirits and men ascend and descend, but only through him, the first one to do so, because, as the Gospel says, no one has ascended to heaven if not he who descended from heaven. Do we not understand the mediator as one who maintains relations with both sides?

But here there is more than a mediator: here is the Son, true God and true man. His eternity is not frozen but draws near and enters among us. It is coming; it has time for us, and we for him, precisely the propitious time, here and now, of the liturgy. We can come close to him with confidence (Heb 4:16) because God and his grace live in him as on their throne: in him God saves. His name is Jesus.

Can we imagine a greater possibility for being liberated from meaninglessness and admitted to the fulfillment of our desire for life after death? Thus, the first Christians were able to pray: "Come, Lord Jesus." And they did not fear in the least that he would come to bring justice. Because he is the judge of the living and the dead, he said that mercy would always triumph in judgment.

If we believed in the love God has for us when we saw him risen, why be afraid? We do not have the spirit of slaves to fall back in fear; rather, we have the Holy Spirit, who has truly made us sons, who brought about our adoption by the Father, we who were once orphans. He has nourished us with the spiritual milk of the Eucharist, making us a "communion of saints". All of this indicates that it is the Eucharist that makes the Church and, before that, her *unity*: "for the visible Church visible unity is more than

'organization'.... Only if she is 'catholic', that is, visibly
one in spite of all her variety, does she correspond to the
demand of the Creed."[6]

In Him We Have Been Made One

Thus, from the many that we were, we have been made
one, one single Church of many churches, one single visible shepherd of many visible shepherds. This is the bond
of unity produced by the liturgy, not by the hierarchy or
organization: it is the bond produced by the presence of
the living Lord, who summons from every part, gathers,
reunifies about his table.

But if, as the Byzantine East says, holy things are given
to the holy, we understand the need for continual purification. Christ, thus, saw that beyond the initial bath of purification, there was also a need for the continual remission
of sins, to make us holy like him who is the Holy One.
These two sacred realities, or sacraments, poured forth from
his pierced heart. God's love did not give up after man's
first fall, and it does not give up in the face of continual
falls, because it does not want the death of the sinner but
that he convert and live.

It is the Spirit who continually rouses, who moves the
heart: he is the place in which the Church acts in the world.
And she herself must not forget that her "action" as the
holy people is always and above all liturgical, mysterious,
sacramental, because she is *of* God; she is the holy people *of*
God; she is completely relative to him. It is precisely this
and nothing else—no ideological project of liberation or

[6] Ibid., p. 346.

values, no pastoral or human project—that makes her totally for the world. Worship always reminds us that it is God who unifies, not our organizing; it is God who grants communion, not our attempts to build. The Church is a gift to be received, period.

Precisely for this reason, it is the sacramentality of the Church, affirmed by Vatican II, that makes her a concrete sign and instrument of unity among men: "A Church without sacraments would be an empty organization, and sacraments without a Church would be rites without meaning or inner cohesion." [7] Holiness—like unity—is a gift to the Church that comes down from above. Sin can stain her, but it cannot deform her. The saints are the indefectible truth of Christianity. They do not separate themselves from sinners; rather, they mix with them, like Jesus, and redeem them with love. They imitate God, who did not isolate himself in his holiness but abased himself in our filth. Saints like Francis carried and sustained the Church. But one cannot sustain unless he also bears with humility: to bear, one must be on the inside of what is handed down. This distinguishes true from false reform of the Church, just as it distinguishes true from false reform of the liturgy: without proud criticism and bitter presumption, it does not throw off the past but maintains it in continuity and, thus, renews it. Nevertheless, whoever truly believes will never cede too much importance to ecclesiastical, liturgical, or pastoral reforms; rather, he will live from that which the Church has always been, namely, from the faith of the simple. In reality, the Church lives in us and not as an object outside of us: here the unity and holiness of the Church, generated

[7] Ibid., p. 338.

in the liturgy, join together with her catholicity: the mention of the pope and the bishop in the Eucharist demonstrate and nourish catholicity.

Christ Is the True Celebrant

Divine worship, we have already said—but it is worthwhile to repeat it—happens only through, with, and in Jesus Christ. If it were otherwise, it would not reach God the Father, to adore him, nor would it touch us, to sanctify us. The worship is not done by us. Pius XII already clarified this in his encyclical *Mediator Dei*. No one can speak of liturgy without beginning with Christ, who is constituted *mediator between God and man*, or without understanding it as the supreme and continuous manifestation of this mediation.

He is the *meeting place* between God and man and makes of the liturgy the culmination of the Church's life and the font of every grace. The work of Christ's redemption is reproposed in an analogous way in the liturgical constitution *Sacrosanctum concilium*.[8]

According to *Mediator Dei*, there is a second essential element of the Catholic liturgy:

> Along with the Church, therefore, her Divine Founder is present at every liturgical function: Christ is present at the august sacrifice of the altar both in the person of His minister and above all under the eucharistic species. He is present in the sacraments, infusing into them the power which makes them ready instruments of sanctification. He is present, finally, in prayer of praise and petition we direct to God, as it is

[8] Cf. Second Vatican Council, Constitution on the Sacred Liturgy *Sacrosanctum concilium* (December 4, 1963), nos. 5–6.

written: "Where there are two or three gathered together
in My Name, there am I in the midst of them" (Mt 18:20).[9]

This passage is taken up again in the famous paragraph of
Sacrosanctum concilium on the presence of Christ,[10] with this
sole addition: "He is present in His word, since it is He
Himself who speaks when the holy scriptures are read in
the Church." Just prior to this, the liturgical constitution,
citing the Veronese sacramentary, affirms that Christ is
"Mediator between God and men" and that worship of the
Eucharist is "the fountain-head of genuine Christian
devotion".[11]

The definition of the liturgy as "the worship rendered
by the Mystical Body of Christ in the entirety of its Head
and members"[12] contained in the encyclical of Pius XII is
repeated in no. 7 of the Constitution on the Liturgy. The
liturgy is the work of Christ, head and members. The Church
intervenes but as subordinated to Christ, who is the principal celebrant. It goes without saying that the priest is the
instrument in the hands of the true celebrant, Christ, for
the salvation of the people. So expressions such as the "celebrating assembly" should not be used injudiciously.[13] Defining the liturgy as the *summit and source*—the celebrated
hendiadys of *Sacrosanctum concilium*[14]—would make no sense
without the presence of Jesus Christ, who came into the
world to be with us always until the end. If, however, we

[9] Pius XII, Encyclical on the Sacred Liturgy *Mediator Dei* (November 20,
1947), no. 20.

[10] *Sacrosanctum concilium*, no. 7.

[11] *Mediator Dei*, no. 5.

[12] Ibid., no. 20.

[13] Congregation for Divine Worship and the Discipline of the Sacraments, Instruction *Redemptionis sacramentum* (March 25, 2004), no. 42.

[14] *Sacrosanctum concilium*, no. 10.

ask committed laypeople, priests, and bishops the definition of the liturgy, they will answer, not with the first,[15]
but with the second definition[16] given by the liturgical constitution. It seems that theologians and liturgists in the postconciliar period have forgotten the Council's first definition
of the liturgy. But it is thanks to the first definition that the
"source and summit" definition—also used by Benedict XVI
in *Sacramentum caritatis*[17]—has its meaning. But we must
also ask ourselves why the first definition has fallen into
disuse. Perhaps because the second lends itself more easily
to the idea that the liturgy is made by us ... with all the
consequences that come from it! Did Vatican II endorse
that idea?

Cardinal Ratzinger, discussing the ecclesiology of *Lumen gentium*, notes that in treating the liturgy before everything
else, Vatican II established the general framework of its
decrees. Talking about the liturgy means talking about God:
"At the beginning there is adoration and, therefore, God."
So, it is impossible to claim that a principally human concept of the liturgy—the arrangement of the liturgy—is the
Council's true intention. The Greek word *ekklesia* comes
from the verb *kaleo* and the corresponding Hebrew *qahal*.
The Church's liturgy is not a spontaneous gathering of people who celebrate the divinity in its own way; nor is it a
congregation organized by the faithful. It is convoked by
God: "The Church is guided by prayer, by the mission of
glorifying God. By its nature, ecclesiology is connected with
the liturgy.... In the history of the post-Conciliar period,

---

[15] Ibid., no. 7.

[16] Ibid., no. 10.

[17] Benedict XVI, Post-synodal Apostolic Exhortation *Sacramentum caritatis*
(February 22, 2007), nos. 3, 17, 70, 76, 83, 93.

the Constitution on the Liturgy was certainly no longer understood from the viewpoint of the basic primacy of adoration, but rather as a recipe book of what we can do with the Liturgy. . . . The more we make it for ourselves, the less attractive it is, because everyone perceives clearly that the essential focus on God has increasingly been lost." [18]

[18] J. Ratzinger, "The Ecclesiology of the Constitution on the Church, Vatican II, *Lumen gentium*", in *L'Osservatore Romano*, English ed., no. 38 (September 19, 2001), p. 5.

III

THE BATTLE OVER LITURGICAL REFORM

The Liturgy Must Be Understood Again in Every Generation

There is a battle taking place over the liturgy. The focus of the forces that gave rise to the liturgical movement at the beginning of the twentieth century was the ancient Roman Rite. The bone of contention today has nothing to do with this. Nevertheless, Joseph Ratzinger reassures us that the struggle for the right interpretation and the worthy celebration of the sacred liturgy is necessary in every generation.[1] Hence, like the *motu proprio* that restores the use of the old Mass, the intention of "coming to an interior reconciliation in the heart of the Church"[2] implies not only healing the formal schism of the Lefebvrists, but also overcoming the break brought about during the reform of the liturgy, opposing the new rite to the old one. Can we ignore this invitation if we truly love the Church and the sacred liturgy?

[1] Foreword to U. M. Lang's *Turning Towards the Lord: Orientation in Liturgical Prayer* (San Francisco: Ignatius Press, 2004), pp. 9–13.

[2] Letter of Pope Benedict XVI to the Bishops on the Occasion of the Publication of the Apostolic Letter "Motu Proprio Data" *Summorum pontificum* on the Use of the Roman Liturgy Prior to the Reform of 1970 (July 7, 2007).

Now, if those who love or have discovered the preceding liturgical tradition must be persuaded "of [the] value and holiness" of the new rite, all others must reflect on the fact that "in the history of the liturgy there is growth and progress, but no rupture. What earlier generations held as sacred remains sacred and great for us too, and it cannot be all of a sudden entirely forbidden or even considered harmful." [3] The words of Benedict XVI recall others:

> Indeed, though we are sorely grieved to note, on the one hand, that there are places where the spirit, understanding or practice of the sacred liturgy is defective, or all but inexistent, We observe with considerable anxiety and some misgiving, that elsewhere certain enthusiasts, over-eager in their search for novelty, are straying beyond the path of sound doctrine and prudence. Not seldom, in fact, they interlard their plans and hopes for a revival of the sacred liturgy with principles which compromise this holiest of causes in theory or practice, and sometimes even taint it with errors touching Catholic faith and ascetical doctrine. [4]

These words were written by Pius XII in the introduction to *Mediator Dei*. The logic is the same: Tradition is necessary and innovation ineluctable, and both are in the nature of the ecclesial body as in the human body. They do not oppose each other but are complementary and interdependent. For this reason, it does not make sense to be extreme innovators or traditionalists. If anything, there is a need to meet and compare without prejudice and with great charity.

Mediator Dei, published on November 24, 1947, by the Servant of God Pius XII, is the most important doctrinal

[3] Ibid.

[4] Pius XII, Encyclical on the Sacred Liturgy *Mediator Dei* (November 20, 1947), no. 8.

document on the liturgy prior to the Second Vatican Council; without it, the Constitution on the Sacred Liturgy, published just sixteen years later, on December 4, 1963, cannot be completely understood. It is the principal source with regard to the classical setting and doctrinal content and the rule and measure for ancient and new liturgical demands. Reading the encyclical seventy years after its promulgation, one is helped to overcome the prejudice toward the so-called "preconciliar Church" and a pope whom his successor John XXIII called "Doctor optimus, Ecclesiae sanctae lumen, divinae legis amator" in his first Christmas radio address in 1958.[5] These are the three titles conferred on doctors of the Church by a liturgical antiphon in the Roman Missal.

Pius XII did not limit himself to enunciating doctrine through the encyclical but followed it up with reforms: the permission to use vernacular alongside the Latin for some parts of liturgical rites in those European and Latin American countries where Catholic unity was not in danger; permitting local ordinaries to allow the celebration of Masses after midday (1957), rediscovering the liturgical day; the revision of the norms for the eucharistic fast (1953) and instructions for the renewal of sacred music, following in the footsteps of Pius X. It is well known that already in 1946, "Pius XII instituted a commission for the general reform of the liturgy, which would begin work in 1948 and which, in 1959, would merge into the liturgical preparatory commission for the Council. It is not out of place, therefore, to claim that preparation for Vatican II's Constitution on the

---

[5] *Discorsi, Messaggi, Colloqui del Santo Padre Giovanni XXIII*, vol. 1: *Primo anno del pontificato: 28 ottobre 1958 28 ottobre 1959* (Vatican City: Tipografia poliglotta vaticana, 1961–1967), p. 101.

Liturgy began in 1948, taking its cue from the encyclical." [6] Unlike the work of all the other commissions, the in-depth preparatory work of this commission did not turn out to be a failure. All of this was launched by the encyclical *Mediator Dei* and would earn the great pontiff who authored it the title of *divini cultus instaurator*. The encyclical still constitutes a measure for comparison in the debate between tradition and innovation.

Pius XII, reconnecting with the constitution *Divini cultus* of his predecessor Pius XI, observes that the ecclesiastical hierarchy "has not been slow—keeping the substance of the Mass and sacraments carefully intact—to modify what it deemed not altogether fitting, and to add what appeared more likely to increase the honor paid to Jesus Christ and the august Trinity, and to instruct and stimulate the Christian people to greater advantage." [7] In fact, the liturgy is composed of divine and human elements: "[T]he human components admit of various modifications, as the needs of the age, circumstance and the good of souls may require, and as the ecclesiastical hierarchy, under guidance of the Holy Spirit, may have authorized. . . . Hence likewise it happens from time to time that certain devotions long since forgotten are revived and practiced anew." [8] This is the criterion that guided Pius XII in the restoration of the rite of Holy Week, bringing back into use ancient traditions that would be acknowledged by the conciliar constitution.[9]

---

[6] A. Tornielli, *Pio XII: Eugenio Pacelli, un uomo sul trono di Pietro* (Milan: Mondadori, 2007), p. 510.

[7] *Mediator Dei*, no. 49; cf. Pius XI, Apostolic Constitution *Divini cultus* (December 20, 1928).

[8] *Mediator Dei*, no. 50.

[9] Cf. Second Vatican Council, Constitution on the Sacred Liturgy *Sacrosanctum concilium* (December 4, 1963), no. 50.

Pope Paul VI succeeded further in applying it in the 1965 edition of the Roman Missal, when he preserved the ancient Mass, removing later duplications from it. This criterion then came back into fashion with Benedict XVI's *motu proprio Summorum pontificum.*

According to *Mediator Dei*, that criterion presides over the evolution of rites but without falling into antiquarianism (*archeologismo*): "The liturgy of the early ages is most certainly worthy of all veneration. But ancient usage must not be esteemed more suitable and proper, either in its own right or in its significance for later times and new situations, on the simple ground that it carries the savor and aroma of antiquity. The more recent liturgical rites likewise deserve reverence and respect. They, too, owe their inspiration to the Holy Spirit." [10] Liturgical reform, then, according to Pius XII, results from the necessity of things, because the liturgy itself is a form that continually tends to re-form itself in the sense of organic development. The abuses cannot make us question this; thus he points out that the Congregation of Rites exists "to protect the purity of divine worship against abuse".[11] The liturgy is the manifestation of the Church, body and head, an organism that always produces new energies while conserving its fundamental form. All of this would be stressed again by *Sacrosanctum concilium.*[12]

Perhaps it is precisely antiquarianism that has shaped the postconciliar reform, claiming the duty to return to the beginning but rejecting the validity of the path taken by tradition. This is what Prosper Guéranger judged to be

[10] *Mediator Dei*, no. 61.
[11] Ibid., no. 57.
[12] *Sacrosanctum concilium*, no. 21.

problematic and unthinkable about the Protestant liturgical reform.[13]

The Reform Proposed by the Council and Its Implementation

There is no content without form; from the moment God became man, there is no truth that does not have a form that points to him. Does re-form mean improving the form or changing it? The meaning does not seem to be univocal.

According to the Fathers, the Church must always be renewed. But reform cannot be understood as a reconstruction following the tastes of the times. Reform, in Michelangelo's view, is what the artist does to free the image from the material that hinders it: the image is already present in the marble, and one need only eliminate the incrustations that have developed over time. To reform is to remove what obscures until the noble form becomes visible, the countenance of the Church and the countenance of Jesus along with it.

This is an admonition to activists, anxious to change structures and people. Of course, this, too, is necessary, but it is more important to pause to listen to the Spirit. The term "reform", used in reference to the liturgy, might or might not be appropriate. It is appropriate if the form corresponds to the content, but it is not if the form indicates a different content. Consider this example: If the Mass no longer puts us on our knees but only makes us stand or sit, this means that from being a blessing or adoration of God, it has been reduced to a conference or sacred theater. The

---

[13] P. Guéranger, *Institutions liturgiques*, I/2 (Paris: Société Génerale de Librairie Catholique, 1878–1885), pp. 388–407.

Constitution on the Liturgy uses the hendiadys *instaurare* and *fovere*, which means a restoration made with care, but it has been translated thus [in the Italian translation]: "reform and augmentation of the liturgy",[14] "augmentation and renovation",[15] a "careful general reform of the liturgy ... of parts susceptible to change";[16] in fact, there is "a part that is unchangeable because it is of divine institution", over which the Church does not have control.[17] So, reform has become synonymous with transformation and change. This is supposed to be what was done by the Council! But in fact, it did not do this. Nevertheless, the Council is blamed by all those who now make changes to the rite according to their own pleasure, despite the Constitution on the Liturgy's exhortation: "Therefore no other person, even if he be a priest, may add, remove, or change anything in the liturgy on his own authority."[18]

The apostolic letter of John XXIII that accompanied the 1962 Missal affirmed that the fundamental principles of the liturgical reform were to be entrusted to the Council fathers. Now, if we look at the principles established in the Constitution on the Liturgy, we do not see any distortion of the tradition. So, has there been no progress in the understanding of the liturgy? Yes and no—which is the nature of the Church as she moves between tradition and innovation. Certainly the conciliar document does not attribute a "closedness" to the old liturgy, as some eminent ecclesiastics have claimed. But then what does that mean? It maintains that communion in the forms of liturgical prayer comes through

[14] *Sacrosanctum concilium*, nos. 1, 3, 14.
[15] Ibid., no. 43.
[16] Ibid., no. 21.
[17] Ibid.
[18] Ibid., no. 22, 3.

the use of a single rite. The liturgy is a living process, not the product of a specialist's erudition.

Unfortunately, the liturgy has become a battlefield. There are more than a few studies that show this. Among these, we should not omit the one on Ferdinando Cardinal Antonelli, who was a peritus and the secretary of the conciliar commission on the liturgy. From the first meeting, he did not have an enthusiastic opinion of the work: of the change in membership of the commission, or *consilium* (forty-two members), of the incompetence of many of its members, of the thirst for novelty, of the hurried discussions, of the chaotic voting and desire to rush approval, of the instability and uncertainty provoked by the reform that ended up favoring the arbitrary. That among the two hundred advisers there were six Protestants, among whom was Max Thurian, who had an active role in the creation of the new Mass, is not negative in itself—it is necessary to ascertain their concrete influence. Antonelli laments the fact that there were even liturgical experiments. Then he wonders how much the perspective and, consequently, the application of the reform were determined by the critical and intolerant spirit toward the Holy See, the rationalism in the liturgy without any concern for true piety, and says: "I am afraid that one day we will have to say of this reform that which was applied to Urban VIII's reform of the hymns: *accepit latinitas recessit pietas.* In this case it will be: *accepit liturgia recessit devotio.* I would love to be able to deceive myself."[19] The Cardinal maintained that the cause of the

<hr>

[19] N. Giampietro, *The Development of the Liturgical Reform as Seen by Cardinal Ferdinando Antonelli from 1948–1970* (Fort Collins, Colo.: Roman Catholic Books, 2009), p. 170. [A translation of *Il card. Ferdinando Antonelli e gli sviluppi della riforma liturgica dal 1948 al 1970* (Rome: Pontificio Ateneo S. Anselmo, 1998).]

problems was precisely the way the *consilium* was structured and the fact that liturgists were not always theologians, despite the fact that every word and gesture in the liturgy expresses a theological idea.[20] It must be added that haste impeded the necessary historical research. In this regard, I can say that, as part of the commission for the revision of the liturgical propers for the diocese of Bari in the 1980s, I went to Rome to find out the reasons for the reduction of the feast of Saint Nicholas in the Roman Calendar to an optional memorial. I was sent to the Dominican Father Ansgarius Dirks. He did not hide the fact that the decision was based on the old Bollandist research, which almost questions the existence of Nicholas. I wondered how it was possible to make such a decision without consulting more recent research.

But let us return to Antonelli. Because already at that time all theology was in dispute, the current theories fell upon the formula and on the rite with a grave consequence: while the theological discussion continued among the specialists, the formula and rite spread among the people. This is why Antonelli came to define the preparatory research of the reform as desacralization and secularization.[21]

Connected to this is another important theme that emerged in this phase of reform already seen by Paul VI in some tendencies and experiments: for many, liturgical law, which until the Council was seen as something sacred, no longer existed. There is no love for what has been handed down; on the contrary, it is disdained. This is why everyone feels authorized to do as he pleases.[22]

---

[20] Ibid., pp. 191, 196.
[21] Ibid., p. 177.
[22] Ibid., pp. 191–92.

Lastly, we cannot be silent about Cardinal Antonelli's severe judgment about the training of Msgr. Bugnini, who is regarded as the real architect of the liturgical reform,[23] and Cardinal Lercaro, the president of the *consilium*. Those who knew Antonelli say that he did not exaggerate. We cannot forget Paul VI's decision to send Bugnini to Iran as the papal nuncio. There are also the negative judgments expressed by the famous French scholars who served on the *consilium*. It is not by chance that it was in France that the strongest opposition to the reform manifested itself. The fact that still today this reform is the object of conflicting evaluations should suggest prudence: for objective verification, time and archival research are necessary.

In any event, to distinguish the reform from the deformations, we need only confirm whether the two criteria specified by the Constitution on the Liturgy were observed: the rites were to be faithfully preserved in their substance, merely simplified, and—if it be opportune or necessary— certain elements that had been lost were to be restored, based on the tradition of the Fathers.[24] We still perceive worry in John Paul II's 1988 apostolic letter *Vicesimus Quintus Annus*, where he speaks openly of "erroneous applications".[25] In another discussion we might reflect on the criterion for the elimination of repetitions and additions.

The point of the foregoing is to help us rightly to judge the reform, which was necessary and in large part correct in intention, and to undertake the pruning that will bring back the liturgy's bloom. If one grows with the Church and in the Church, one thinks with the Church. The

[23] Ibid., p. 196.

[24] Cf. *Sacrosanctum concilium*, no. 50.

[25] John Paul II, Apostolic Letter *Vicesimus Quintus Annus* (December 4, 1988), no. 13.

Church's reform is guided by a central principle: the mutual enrichment of the ancient and the new—as desired by Pius XII, who spoke of it to the participants in the international liturgical congress, which took place in Assisi, September 18–23, 1956. It was no accident that it was taken up again by Paul VI in the apostolic constitution promulgating the new Missal.

Paul VI's Corrections

Published in April 1969, Paul VI's *Institutio*, or *General Instruction of the Roman Missal*, received a very sharp reaction shortly afterward, namely, the letter to the Pope by Cardinals Ottaviani and Bacci, who subjected the new rite prepared by the experts of the "committee for the implementation of the Sacred Constitution on the Liturgy" to a "brief critical examination".[26] The letter denounced a "surprising departure from the Catholic theology of the Holy Mass" and asked for permission "to continue to have recourse to the fruitful integrity of that *Missale Romanum* of Pius V, so highly lauded by Your Holiness and so profoundly venerated and loved by the entire Catholic world."[27] Many other criticisms were made of the rite and the doctrine.[28] Why?

After the Council had expressed the desire in the Constitution on the Liturgy that the various parts of the Mass be revised "in such a way that the intrinsic nature and purpose of its several parts, as also the connection between

[26] "Breve esame critico del 'Novus Ordo Missae'", http://www.unavox.it/doc14.htm (accessed on August 16, 2010).

[27] Ibid.

[28] Giampietro, *Development of the Liturgical Reform*, pp. 193–94.

them, may be more clearly manifested",[29] at the Synod of Bishops in 1967 a judgment was asked for on the experimental celebration of the so-called "normative Mass" proposed by the *consilium*. According to the letter of Ottaviani and Bacci, of the 187 votes cast, there were 43 *non placet*, many reservations (62 *juxta modum*), and 4 abstentions. But the *Novus Ordo Missae* was promulgated two years later by Paul VI with the apostolic constitution *Missale Romanum*. This step was taken since the reform was considered necessary in order to allow the people to understand the liturgy better. But did the people want the face of the liturgy to be changed? That document states that the issue had been addressed, but in their letter, Ottaviani and Bacci claimed that a tradition had been subverted that had been unchanged in the Church from the time of Gregory the Great, that had been normative from the Missal of Pius V until then.

The letter pointed out the fact that the definition of the Mass had been limited to that of "meal", which does not imply the *real presence* or the reality of sacrifice or the sacramentality of the consecrating priest or the intrinsic value of the eucharistic sacrifice that is independent of the presence of the assembly. In a word, it did not imply any of the essential dogmatic features that define the Mass.

The letter also noted the inexactness of the formula *Memoriale Passionis et Resurrectionis Dominis*, the Mass being the memorial of the one sacrifice, which is redemptive in itself, while the Resurrection is the consequent fruit. It was claimed, among other things, that the ultimate finality of the Mass as a sacrifice of praise to the Most Holy Trinity had disappeared along with the ordinary finality of the

---

[29] *Sacrosanctum concilium*, no. 50.

Mass as propitiatory sacrifice. In regard to the latter, the new Mass, instead of emphasizing the remission of sins of the living and the dead, stressed the nourishment and sanctification of those present.[30] In regard to the essence of the sacrifice, the letter accused the new Mass of no longer explicitly expressing the mystery of the Cross. It identified the cause of this lack of explicitness about the sacrifice as being in the suppression of the central role of the *real presence*, which in the old rite was clearly evident; nor was there any allusion to the permanence of the real presence of Christ in body, blood, soul, and divinity in the transubstantiated species. The word "transubstantiation" was ignored, the very word chosen by Saint Thomas Aquinas *in primis* to indicate the transformation of the bread and wine into the Body and Blood of Jesus Christ, which is accomplished by the efficaciousness of his word and the action of the Holy Spirit.

The letter also criticized the function assigned to the altar, which, with the exclusion of the altar as the place of repose for the Blessed Sacrament, was almost constantly called "table". This would signal an insurmountable dichotomy between the presence in the celebrant of Jesus the eternal High Priest and that same presence realized sacramentally. In the past they had been a single presence. The *Institutio* now recommended that the Blessed Sacrament be kept in a separate place, where the private devotion of the faithful could be expressed, treating the Blessed Sacrament as if it were just any other relic. Thus, on entering a church, one's attention would be drawn, no longer by the tabernacle, but by a table that is stripped bare. Once again, private piety was set in opposition to liturgical piety, and altar was set up

---

[30] Cf. *General Instruction of the Roman Missal*, no. 54.

against altar. In this connection, there is a curious fact that should be considered. The letter of Cardinals Ottaviani and Bacci and Paul VI's apostolic constitution *Missale Romanum* cite respectively two different passages from Pius XII's address to the Assisi congress of 1956: the first states that "separating the tabernacle from the altar is equivalent to separating two things that by the force of their nature should remain unified", and the second holds that the growth of liturgical studies is a salutary movement of the Holy Spirit in the Church. If this movement has indeed occurred, as we believe, can we attribute to it the separation of the tabernacle from the altar where Mass is celebrated?

In short, if this letter did not cause an earthquake, it certainly did have some effect: Paul VI had to stop further publication of the *Institutio*, have it amended, and republish it a year later in May 1970.[31] To see that the two texts are different, one need only compare §7 in the first and second editions. In the 1969 text we read:

> The supper of the Lord, or the Mass, is the holy assembly or gathering of the people of God, who join together, with the priest presiding, to celebrate the memorial of the Lord. For this reason Christ's promise applies in an eminent way

[31] The first edition of the *General Instruction of the Roman Missal* was published on April 6, 1969, along with the *editio typica* of the *Ordo Missae* (cf. International Commission on English in the Liturgy, *Documents on the Liturgy, 1963–1979: Conciliar, Papal, and Curial Texts* [Collegeville, Minn.: Liturgical Press, 1982], pp. 461, 465n). The second, revised version of the *General Instruction* was published with the first *editio typica* of the new Roman Missal on March 26, 1970 (cf. ibid., pp. 461–63, 465n). A third edition of the *General Instruction* was published in 1973, a fourth in 1975, and a fifth in 2002. Each edition, of course, contained various revisions. The text of the first edition of the *General Instruction* is not widely available. One can find the Latin text in *Ordo Missae* (Vatican City: Typis Polyglottis Vaticanis, 1969), pp. 13–76.—TRANS.

to the local gathering of the holy Church: "Where two or
three are gathered in my name, there am I in their midst"
(Mt 18:20).

However, in the 1970 text we find this revised version of §7:

> *In the Mass*, or supper of the Lord, *the people of God is called
> to join together*, with the priest presiding, *who acts in the per-
> son of Christ*, to celebrate the memorial of the Lord, *that is,
> the eucharistic sacrifice.* For this reason Christ's promise applies
> in an eminent way to such a local gathering of the holy
> Church: "Where two or three are gathered in my name,
> there am I in their midst" (Mt 18:20). In fact, in the cel-
> ebration of Mass, in which the sacrifice of the Cross is per-
> petuated, Christ is really present in the very liturgical assembly
> gathered in his name, in the person of the minister, in his
> word, and in a substantial and permanent way in the
> eucharistic species.

The italics show us the important changes to the text that
accompanied the new rite of the Mass. Despite this, we
still hear it repeated today that the Eucharist is a meal, a
claim that has been spread after the time of Luther, because
until that period no one doubted that the Eucharist was
the sacrifice of Christ inasmuch as it commemorated his
death on the Cross.[32]

The criticisms did not cease. Paul VI expected "a happy
spreading of the Catholic faith in our time. Those who take
advantage of the reform, then, to indulge in arbitrary experiments are wasting energy and offending ecclesial sensibility"

---

[32] Cf. J. Ratzinger, "Forma e contenuto della celebrazione eucaristica",
Communio 35 (1977): 1838 (see English translation as the second chapter,
"Form and Content in the Eucharistic Celebration", in part 1 of Joseph
Cardinal Ratzinger, *The Feast of Faith*, trans. Graham Harrison [San Fran-
cisco: Ignatius Press, 1986], 33–49).

(General Audience, August 22, 1973). But many observed that
the incentives for the arbitrary experiments stemmed from the
weak points of the reform. Did not the great number of options
provided by the new rubrics in regard to the liturgical celebration, which left so much to local discretion, end up con-
fusing ideas about Catholic doctrine on the Mass? Paul VI was
convinced that the liturgical reform implemented after the
Council truly introduced and *firmly* supported the indica-
tions of *Sacrosanctum concilium* (cf. Speech to the Sacred Col-
lege, June 22, 1973). But the arbitrary experimentation
continued and, on the contrary, heightened nostalgia for the
old rite. At the consistory on June 27, 1977, the Pope admon-
ished the "partisans" for improvisation, banality, frivolity, and
profanation, calling on them in a severe tone to keep to the
established norms so as not to compromise the *regula fidei*,
dogma, ecclesiastical discipline, the *lex credendi* and *orandi*. But
he also called upon the traditionalists to recognize that the
changes made to the sacred rites did not touch their substance.

Despite this, there are those who claim that the liturgical
reform desired by Vatican II was opposed and progressively
derailed by the Roman Curia to the point of asserting that
it constituted the basis for the convoking of the Council
and the inspiration for its objectives. There are also those
who maintain that not only did the Council envision a new
way to understand and perform the liturgy but that Pius V's
Church and liturgy were something different from the
Church and liturgy from which we had learned to believe,
live, and pray the past forty years. In sum, another Church
was born with the Council! If such interpreters are right,
then we must conclude that another liturgy has also been
born and that the liturgy of the Catholic Church has not
been renewed! The interpretation of the Council, of its
contents, of its authoritativeness, has become a point of

conflict between conservatives and innovators, the former relativizing it and denying the necessity of the tradition's development, and the latter absolutizing it and isolating it from the tradition.

Antiquarianism then led to idealizing the first millennium—except for prayer facing east! and ostracizing the second millennium—the medieval and modern periods—as the quintessence of devotionalism and clericalism. It was forgotten that the development of dogma occurs in the living tradition of which the liturgy is an essential part. Antonelli, taking his cue from the historical and practical aspect of the *confiteor* at the beginning of the Mass, observes in a meeting of the *consilium*: "It is to be remembered that anyone who wishes to revive institutions which have ceased to exist and are no longer effective simply because they existed in the past smacks of archeologism, as indeed do those who refuse to accept useful elements simply because they did not exist in antiquity." [33] What Antonelli says about the revision of the baptismal rite is striking: "I had to observe that where one would expect to highlight original sin, for instance when there is the little homily of catechetical character, it would appear that all trace of it had vanished. I dislike this new, vapid, theological mentality." [34] What Paul VI did not want to happen, happened. Instead of secular humanism opening up to the Church, the religion of man who makes himself God penetrated the Church. [35]

To get at the heart of the matter, the primary cause is the entrance of Rahner's "anthropological turn" into the liturgy. The liturgy has become a community affair, an affair of

[33] Giampietro, *Development of the Liturgical Reform*, p. 170.
[34] Ibid., p. 178.
[35] Cf. Concluding Homily of the Ninth Session of Vatican Council II, December 7, 1965.

the ideas and personal experiences of its members, in which, through its creativity, the community represents itself to itself and the purpose of divine worship—the encounter with the Lord in the Church—disappears. How has it happened that in using "engaged language" in the liturgy, contemporary man has removed himself from the Church?

In the 1974 apostolic letter *Apostolorum limina* for the inauguration of the Holy Year, Paul VI notes: "We regard it as extremely opportune that this work be reexamined and receive new developments in such a way that, basing itself on what has been strongly confirmed by the authority of the Church, one would see everywhere what is valid and legitimate and the work would continue the application with still greater zeal, guided by the norms and methods counseled by pastoral prudence and a true piety." [36] In the postconciliar period perhaps there was too much haste and no time taken for reflection. Thus, things were eliminated without appropriate discernment. For some, everything that was old seemed bad, while for others, everything that was new seemed bad. Today we need to proceed with care; otherwise, claiming that all or almost all of the reform was negative or positive, we will make the same mistake. The whole liturgical reform—including the parts already implemented—can be reevaluated in the light of the true spirit of the liturgy. [37]

If we cannot say that liturgical reform has not taken off, we can certainly say that it has flown low, zigzagging and not always in line with the twentieth-century liturgical movement or, above all, with the restoration of Pius XII, making chance landings in various airports. There are, therefore,

[36] Paul VI, Apostolic Letter *Apostolorum limina* (May 23, 1974), no. IV.

[37] Cf. chapter 9 of *The Ratzinger Report: An Exclusive Interview on the State of the Church*, trans. S. Attanasio and G. Harrison (San Francisco: Ignatius Press, 1985).

obscurities that need to be cleared up with respect to how it was carried out. Did it go beyond the Council's intentions? This is why a cease-fire was called in the battle: the *usus antiquior* has returned as a mirror alongside the new form of the rite. If some new ritual forms have seemed to give in to the spirit of the world, a calm deepening and revision or restoration of some of the old forms could remove any fear.

IV

THE POPE CALLS A CEASE-FIRE

The *motu proprio Summorum pontificorum* is a specific legislative act, as the document itself and the letter that Benedict XVI wrote to accompany it make clear.

To use a theological expression, the *motu proprio* constitutes an important exercise of his *munus regendi*, that is, the power to govern proper to the Catholic hierarchy with the pope as its head. The "doctrinal" objective of the pontifical document can be summarized in three points: to facilitate internal reconciliation in the Church; to offer everyone the possibility of participating in the "extraordinary form" considered as a precious treasure that should not be lost; to guarantee the right of the people of God—the priests, laity, and groups who ask for it—to the use of the "extraordinary form".

The pontifical commission *Ecclesia Dei* is charged with overseeing and promoting its implementation in dialogue with bishops, priests, and lay faithful. Nevertheless, further clarifications are expected through a specific instruction.

Meanwhile, everyone can learn the Holy Father's reasons for his actions as they are set forth in the letter to the bishops.

The Motu Proprio's *Key Doctrinal and Disciplinary Points*

To dispel the fear that the restoration of the Roman Missal in its last preconciliar edition of 1962 undermined the authority of the Council on the basis of which Paul VI published the new Missal, Benedict XVI's letter states that it is a matter of *two versions* (*stesure*), consistent with the development of the one rite. There are precedents for this. In fact, those who know the history of liturgical books are aware that when they were reprinted they were amended and enriched with formulas for Masses, blessings, and so on. So, the two Missals do not belong to *two rites*. It is an answer to those—both traditionalists and innovators—who claimed that the old Roman Rite died with the liturgical reform and that a new, totally different, rite was born, that there was a real break.[1]

When in 1970 the revised rite of the Mass was published, it was thought that the 1962 Missal would now be used by only a few and that the problem would be resolved case by case. This is not what happened, the Holy Father says: the use of the 1962 Missal went well beyond traditionalist groups and the elderly. "[I]t has clearly been demonstrated that young persons too have discovered this liturgical form, felt its attraction and found in it a form of encounter with the Mystery of the Most Holy Eucharist, particularly suited to them."[2] The need for juridical regulation through the *motu proprio* emerged also to help the bishops exercise, in a Catholic way, the task of moderators of the liturgy in particular churches.

---

[1] On this issue see M. Gagliardi, *Introduzione al Mistero eucharistico: Dottrina liturgia, devozione* (Rome: San Clemente, 2007), pp. 320–22.

[2] Letter of Pope Benedict XVI to the Bishops on the Occasion of the Publication of the Apostolic Letter "Motu Proprio Data" *Summorum pontificum* on the Use of the Roman Liturgy Prior to the Reform of 1970 (July 7, 2007).

To dispel another fear, of disorder and divisions in parish communities, the Pope noted that it had little basis, since the use of the old Missal presupposes a certain liturgical formation and access to the Latin language—things that are not typically part of the reality of the faithful. Thus the new Missal remains valid for ordinary use and the old for extraordinary use. Excesses are possible on the part of faithful attached to the old and on the part of those who always and in every case love novelty, as do some "creative" priests. The way to avoid these excesses is in the use of both forms of the rite by both groups, as has been counseled—not ordered. This will allow them to see that these forms must mutually enrich or contaminate (in a positive sense) each other. The new form, especially, will recover sacrality and reverence "in harmony with the liturgical directives" contained in it, which will "bring out the spiritual richness and theological depth of this Missal". We know that this is what occurred in the history of the Eastern and Western liturgies between, for example, the Antiochene and the Byzantine liturgies or the Roman and Alexandrian liturgies.

After having demonstrated the baselessness of the fears, the letter furnishes the positive reason for the *motu proprio*, that is, the doctrinal and pastoral objective that those who put on the name of Christ cannot but have at heart: "an interior reconciliation in the heart of the Church ... [making] every effort to enable ... all those who truly desire unity to remain in that unity or to attain it anew." Did Jesus not pray that they be unified so that the world would see and believe? Who could object? And yet there are those who do not agree with the following statement in the letter: "There is no contradiction between the two editions of the Roman Missal. In the history of the liturgy there is growth and progress, but no rupture. What earlier generations held as sacred, remains sacred and great for us too, and it cannot be all of a sudden entirely forbidden or even considered harmful. It behooves all of us to preserve the riches which have developed in the Church's faith and prayer, and to give them their proper place." We have here an admonition addressed to both groups, directing them to find balance again.

In regard to the bishop's authority, nothing is taken away: he must oversee and moderate. In this case, the term "moderator" is quite meaningful. But the role must be performed "in full harmony, however, with all that has been laid down by the new norms of the Motu Proprio." We might say that this moderation consists in facilitating the mutual enrichment of which we spoke; in fact, at the end of the letter it says that those who celebrate with the old Missal should also celebrate with the new. It is not a command but a suggestion; respect for both uses, however, is obligatory. Consequently, those who celebrate according to the old use must avoid delegitimizing the new use, and vice versa. So, it is not permissible to refuse to celebrate the new form because of prejudgments (*per partito preso*). It would not be a sign of communion to refuse, for instance, to concelebrate with a bishop who intends to use the new Missal.

The Church is not a hereditary monarchy, and, therefore, the Pope, broadly speaking, is not bound by the decisions of his predecessor, since new situations always arise. Nevertheless, the Holy Father subsequently asked for a report from the bishops so as to be apprised of the situation. Thus, an opportunity was given to the interested communities of lay faithful or religious attached to the tradition—above all those who have remained in communion with Rome—to show with their actions that they truly desire to achieve concord and reconciliation. It would be paradoxical if the Mass, whose culminating moment is the Eucharist—the sacrament of unity and peace par excellence—were to become a sign of division, of discord, and thus the portent of conflict. It must be added that for the followers of Archbishop Lefebvre, as for the proponents of the abuses in the renewed liturgy, this is a time to demonstrate, with great humility and simplicity, their wish to abandon, on the one hand, the positions of separation and to return to full communion with Rome, without any will for revenge, and, on the other hand, the manipulation of the liturgy, which is not private property, and to celebrate it in a Catholic spirit, because it belongs to the whole Church. It would be a sign that the *motu proprio* had brought about an important result, which is what is hoped by the first, namely, that the liberalization of the old rite might be a propaedeutic to full reconciliation, and what is claimed by the second, namely, that the new liturgy contains and develops the ancient one of the Roman sacramentaries.

Beyond ritual forms, it must not be forgotten, as the Holy Father opportunely recalls in the letter, that the substance of the liturgy is the reverence for and adoration of God, that God who is present in the Church. The nature of the liturgy must not be reduced to a disquisition on forms: the important question is whether the liturgy, old or new, truly helps to render to God the worship owed him in the most consonant and appropriate forms, in spirit and truth.

A Little History

It is curious that both the enthusiasts of tradition and the lovers of innovation look to the old: the ones to conserve and the others to renew. Do not the latter claim that the new liturgy has restored ancient rites that had fallen into disuse? Here are two examples, among others: the prayer of the faithful and concelebration. It is right, then, that the letter does a little history to bring some doctrinal principles of the Catholic liturgy into synthesis.

a. The popes, from the beginning to today, have been caretakers of the worship that the Church must offer to the divine majesty, that it might be a worship *worthy* "to the praise and glory of his name" and "for the good of all his holy Church". There is a retrieval of the principle to be observed[3] in regard to the concordance of the doctrine, signs, and customs of the particular church with the universal Church, "that the Church's law of prayer correspond to her law of faith".

b. The most prominent figure is Saint Gregory the Great, who, as the Pope points out in *Summorum pontificum* "commanded that the form of the sacred liturgy as celebrated in Rome (concerning both the Sacrifice of the Mass and the Divine Office) be conserved". Since he in a certain sense entrusted the Benedictines with the spread of the Gospel and the implementation of the Rule of Saint Benedict, in which it is recommended that "nothing should be placed before the work of God",[4] in this way he allowed the Roman liturgy to enrich many people with faith, piety, and culture.

After Gregory, other pontiffs continued this work. In particular, Saint Pius V, who, following the directives of the Council of Trent "renewed the entire liturgy of the Church,

---

[3] Cf. *General Instruction of the Roman Missal*, 5th ed. (2002), no. 397.
[4] Rule of Saint Benedict, no. 43.

oversaw the publication of liturgical books amended and 'renewed in accordance with the norms of the Fathers', and provided them for the use of the Latin Church".[5] The Roman Missal was central among these texts.

c. After the updating and defining of the rites and liturgical books on the part of other pontiffs, such as Clement VIII and Urban VIII, we come to the general reform of the twentieth century with Saint Pius X, Benedict XV, Pius XII, and Blessed John XXIII. Finally, Vatican Council II "expressed a desire that the respectful reverence due to divine worship should be renewed and adapted to the needs of our time".[6] Paul VI, "moved by this desire ... in 1970 reformed and partly renewed liturgical books for the Latin Church".[7] They were well received by the bishops, priests, and faithful of the world. John Paul II revised the *editio typica* of the new Roman Missal, publishing its third edition. The purpose of such work is the splendor of the liturgy, through worthiness and harmony, as Catholic worship offered to God, one and three.

d. But the fact that "in some regions" no small number of faithful continued to use "the earlier liturgical forms", which had permeated their culture and their spirit, moved John Paul II in 1984 to grant an indult through the Congregation of Divine Worship that gave faculties to use the 1962 Missal; and with the 1988 *motu proprio Ecclesia Dei*, he exhorted the bishops to make "generous use of this power in favor of all

---

[5] Benedict XVI, Apostolic Letter *Summorum pontificum* issued *motu proprio* (July 7, 2007), unofficial Vatican Information Service translation of the official Latin text.

[6] Ibid.

[7] Ibid.

the faithful who so desired".[8] This is the prior event, along with the insistence of many faithful and the results of the discussion that took place in a consistory on March 23, 2006, that led Benedict XVI, after "having reflected deeply upon all aspects of the question, invoked the Holy Spirit and trusting in the help of God", to establish in twelve articles the norms to be followed by bishops and faithful.

In summary:

1. The Church has only one *lex orandi*, but it is expressed in two ways that do not lead to any division in the *lex credendi* of the Church. In other words, there is one rite with two forms: ordinary and extraordinary. The earlier Roman Missal was never abrogated.

2. In its essential structure, the old Mass, above all the Roman Canon, is that of Gregory the Great. It is directed to everyone, and any priest can celebrate it without any permission from the Holy See or the diocesan bishop. It must be offered to all, and anyone may participate in it without any limit on the number. The same holds for Baptism, Matrimony, Penance, and Extreme Unction in the ancient rite. The old formulae for Confirmation and Holy Orders remain valid. Thus, too, the Divine Office.

3. The readings may be proclaimed in the vernacular according to the rubrics for the 1962 Missal.

4. The faithful who have not obtained satisfaction from the parish priest may speak to the bishop. If he is not able to

---

[8] Ibid.

provide for them, they may turn to the pontifical *Ecclesia Dei* commission, which exercises the Holy See's authority, overseeing the observance and application of these directives.

So, the *motu proprio* sets the old rite alongside the new. It does not replace it; it is optional, not obligatory. It does not take away but adds. Thus it expresses unity in variety. It is an enrichment that must heal the wounds caused by the fracture in the communion and lead to reconciliation within the Church, overcoming the interpretations of the Council that favored liturgical deformations. Finally, the osmosis between the old and the new rite will avoid individualism with respect to the former and communitarianism with respect to the latter if in each person it incites the memory of Christ from whom the communion of all flows.

Misinterpretations of the Papal Action

After the publication of the *motu proprio*, certain clerical, religious, and lay supporters of liturgical experimentation proposed not a few mistaken interpretations: they presupposed that until Vatican II the Church had been in a frozen state and only with the Council did she manage to move; thus, they opposed progress to the tradition. But does *tradere* not mean transmitting something from one generation to the next, a content from one age to another? And in this context, does it not have to do with the whole complex of liturgical gestures and texts? Can one not say that tradition inevitably implies progress? If the postconciliar liturgical reform intended to propose to priests the possibility of choosing what in the tradition to keep and what to throw out, we would be dealing with a heresy. But if we consider only the numerous *licet* and *possit* that appear in the liturgical rubrics of the Missal of Paul VI, we will see that this is not the case. Benedict XVI's *motu proprio* wants to offer more choices, that is, it wants to reaffirm that the ancient liturgy was never abolished insofar as it is fully Catholic. One can say that John XXIII's updating of the 1962 Missal cannot be opposed to Paul VI's eight years later. The riches of the two must be held together. The old Mass belongs to the *regula fidei* as its extraordinary and not exceptional expression alongside the ordinary and normal expression; indeed, we have "two forms of the ancient Roman Rite".

The authority of the Council must not be eroded, and the liturgical reform must not be put in question either by those who are most attached to the old form codified in the 1962 Missal or by those who prefer the 1970 Missal. It is obvious that what is ordinary is not equal to what is extraordinary, but it would be strange if we were to live only from the first and had no need of the second, just as the ferial is ordinary and the feast is extraordinary. Thus it is erroneous to hold, as some do, that this new decree was promulgated for the traditionalists, because the intention of the *motu proprio* is that everyone in the Church look at the old rite, indeed, that priests may celebrate it and the faithful participate in it. A Christian of the East who goes to church can attend the rite of Chrysostom or of Basil, according to the liturgical time. Analogously, Catholic dioceses should not limit themselves to waiting for requests but should offer the possibility.

Why claim that those who love the old rite are ignorant of Scripture and of the liturgy and affected by devotionalism as if those who participate in the new liturgy were more educated and free of sentimentalism? Just read the essays and articles by liturgists to see their dissatisfaction and complaints about the faithful participating in the new rite, too.

On the other hand, it is not only traditionalists who take the liturgy as a badge of identity to affirm Catholic fundamentalism but also many progressives, who wish to claim an autonomy of the Protestant and anti-globalization sort (consider the peace banners hoisted in front of churches and placed before altars). The political and cultural instrumentalization of the Mass or its reduction to folklore or spectacle occurs on both sides.

Claiming that it is only a few irremediably nostalgic people and groups with an infantile sensibility who follow the *motu proprio* or that the hundreds of places in Europe and elsewhere where the Mass is celebrated according to the old rite are irrelevant implies that the small communities of Eastern Rite Catholics, who live in an analogous diaspora, should also disappear along with their rites. Is it an evangelical criterion that guides us to make judgments based on quantity? And then, how on earth is it the case that the old rite is sought out especially by young people—as the Pope says in the *motu proprio*—who have never known it? Is it reducible to personal taste? Leaving aside the extreme cases of "beat Masses" where the priest dances, "revolutionary Masses", as in Colombia, where the priest, wearing a stole, holds a machine gun in one hand and the Missal in the other, "circus Masses" where the priest wears a clown mask, "picnic Masses", and so on, does it not also happen that during the Mass the priest substitutes non-biblical readings for the prescribed ones, changes an article in the Creed, inserts words into the Eucharistic Prayer? To what are these things to be attributed if not to personal choice? Do those who do such things interpret the liturgical reform properly? Or do they succumb to subjectivism and relativism, to the point of caricaturing and profaning the sacred liturgy? It is this—and not the *motu proprio*—that has led to anarchy, taking the liturgy away from the authority of the bishops and pitting the faithful against rebellious priests. Some have proposed a kind of "conscientious objection", as though the Mass were the property of the priest and the community: this—and not the *motu proprio*—is a direct attack on the heart of Vatican II and the new rite.

If we argue that unity with traditionalists should not be bought at too great a cost, the same must also go for ecumenical unity with Protestants and Orthodox, which some have sought with great ardor but not with great clarity. If someone claims that a theological problem cannot have a liturgical answer, then why the concern for what the Orthodox think about the lack of an epiclesis to the Holy Spirit in the Roman Canon? It is admitted that this is the case, but Louis Bouyer and others have demonstrated otherwise. What a contradiction!

So, we should be concerned not only with declarations by schismatic traditionalists about the *motu proprio* but also with remonstrations by eminent but disobedient innovators. Finally, to derive the superiority of one missal over the other solely from the use to which it is put would mean that the liturgy for Ordinary Time would be regarded as better than that for the special liturgical seasons. This would be analogous to regarding the Liturgy of Saint John Chrysostom in the Eastern Rite, which is ordinarily celebrated, as superior to the Liturgy of Saint Basil or that of the Presanctified Gifts, which are celebrated only on special occasions. One would be mistaken to use similar reasoning in refusing to celebrate in the ordinary form or in the extraordinary form. Either way one would fall into disobedience and formalism.

If it were true that the old rite privileges a personal devotional and aesthetic dimension, then it must be observed that the new rite is excessive with respect to communitarianism, participationism without devotion, and the spectacular.

It is further claimed that the old form did not permit spiritual worship, which is why it was necessary to move toward the liturgy that came out of the conciliar reform. But there is a contradiction here, because in this way one falls into opposing the pre- and postconciliar, an opposition that was denied and attributed to the traditionalists. The Tridentine liturgy is then accused of being "Dionysian". But in what sense? In that of Dionysius-Bacchus or of Dionysus the Areopagite? If the latter, then what would the Byzantine liturgy be, with its redundant richness, given the influence that the mysterious fourth-century author has had on it? Comparative studies show that the Roman liturgy in its preconciliar form was much closer to the Eastern liturgy than the current form. So, one must be careful in coining epithets and in applying Augustinian ecclesiology to the reformed liturgy; otherwise it would come out battered, given the abuses in the realization of that liturgy.

If the old liturgy was a "covered fresco", the new has threatened to destroy this fresco by the aggressive techniques used in restoring it. But the *motu proprio* sets before us the centuries-old rite of the Catholic Church, which the new rite must not fear to look upon in order to recover some essential elements. It is true that Pope Paul VI intended simply to restore the rite of Saint Pius V, that is, the liturgy of Saint Gregory, but, in a first phase, unfortunately, the experts got the upper hand, "fabricating" something else. When the Pope became aware of it, we saw what happened: the bulls had already escaped from the pen, as one says. Precisely that blunder caused the fracture because it made clear that everything had not gone the right way.

Now Benedict XVI begins from the same point. The old form of the Mass belongs to the Catholic ecclesial tradition and cannot be censured but must in fact be used together with the new. After all, the concept of the Latin liturgy, which includes the Roman liturgy, indicates that there are multiple ritual forms: the Roman is the principal form, with the traits of universality and sobriety that permitted it to be adopted by the majority of local churches in the global North and South besides in the West and even in a small part of the East alongside the Eastern liturgies; moreover, at the time of Pius V there were still rites that characterized local churches and religious orders, and these were not suppressed if they were two hundred or more years old. So why are some surprised by the restoration of the old form if it has still remained forty years after the liturgical reform? If the traditionalists have clung to the Missal of Pius V, it is also because the innovators have gone beyond that of Paul VI in the name of creativity. If it were true that all of what is in the Missal of Pius V is included in that of Paul VI, who only updated and added to it, without rejecting or omitting anything fundamental in the celebration of the eucharistic mystery, this would mean that the prayers and prefaces from the fifth and seventh centuries are found in both. So why oppose the two to each other?

Unfortunately, the Missal of Paul VI does not contain everything of the Missal of Pius V—especially if one considers the editions in the national languages. Furthermore, it has changed many things in the old Missal and added new texts. In the new Missal the meaning of the Latin text is often censored and changed.[9] Klaus Gamber, one of the best and most knowledgeable historians of the liturgy and a

---

[9] Lorenzo Bianchi has documented a "total suppression of the expressions related to sin and evil (*peccata nostra, imminentia pericula, mentis nostrae tenebrae*) and those related to the necessity of redemption and forgiveness (*puriores, mundati, reparatio nostra, purificatis mentibus*)" (*Liturgia: Memoria o Istruzioni per l'uso?* [Casale Monferrato: Piemme, 2002], p. 59).

specialist in the ancient Roman liturgy and Eastern Rites, has pronounced a very severe judgment on the new Missal.[10]

Joseph Ratzinger has observed that before the liturgical movement and before Vatican II the liturgy was like a fresco that was well preserved; to be sure, it was covered by soot and plaster, which were removed by the worthy labor of restorers in the Council, who brought the splendor of the original to light.[11] The success of the interventions, nevertheless, increased the audacity of the restorers, who were unable to restrain themselves even after they had reached the highest point of revealing the liturgy's splendor. Now that he is pope, Benedict XVI has launched an effort at repair with the post-synodal exhortation *Sacramentum caritatis* and with the *motu proprio*.

If in order not to offend the sensibility of our Jewish brothers and sisters, some prefer to speak of the First and Second Testaments instead of the Old and New; analogously, so as not to offend our Christian brothers and sisters, one could speak of the old and new Missals as of the *antiquus* and *novus ordo missae*. It does not occur to Catholics to speak of dialogue, even with those who are so inclined, but, as Giovanni Guareschi says, the only ones who are excluded from "dialogue" are those who are wholly Catholic.[12]

The Eucharist of the Lord remains one, beyond the old and new forms, just as it does in the ancient Eastern liturgies different from our own. As the German scholar Martin

---

[10] Cf. K. Gamber, *La Réforme liturgique en question* (Barroux: Saint Madeleine, 1992), pp. 81–87.

[11] J. Ratzinger, *The Spirit of the Liturgy*, trans. John Saward (San Francisco: Ignatius Press, 2000), pp. 7–8.

[12] Cf. G. Guareschi, "Al di là del bene e del male," in *Don Camillo e i giovani d'oggi* (Milan: Rizzoli, 1969), p. 8.

Mosebach suggests, the *usus antiquior* should be known as the "Liturgy of Saint Gregory the Great", as the Eastern liturgy is known as "the Liturgy of Saint John Chrysostom".

So, the reconciliation called for by Pope Benedict is not a nostalgic undertaking but a recovery of the apostolic tradition and of the spirit of discipline. The proper interior disposition for participating in the liturgy is one of veneration and receptivity. It is not an attitude of "do-it-yourself". Saint Benedict writes: "We must understand how to conduct ourselves in the presence of God and his angels; thus, we must celebrate the liturgy of the hours in such a way that our mind conforms with our words." [13] I reflect often on this phrase, which one can find inscribed in Latin in the Benedictine cloister of Sant'Anselmo on the Aventine in Rome.

[13] Rule of Saint Benedict, no. 19.

V

THE ECCLESIAL CRISIS AND THE DISINTEGRATION OF THE LITURGY

Ecclesial and Liturgical Continuity

According to some, the *motu proprio Summorum pontificum* of Benedict XVI, which once again permits the celebration of the so-called "Tridentine Rite", runs the risk of creating "upheaval" because the ecclesiology of the old Missal is supposedly "incompatible" with that of Vatican II; a bishop has spoken of the *motu "im-proprio"*. Let us consider the validity of such a thesis, taking up the Roman Canon, the Eucharistic Prayer that has remained in the Missal of Paul VI. In it, the priest turns in the first place to the Father and presents the offering "for the holy catholic Church" so that she might be gathered together in unity—as is also prayed in the ancient *Didache*—and so that he might lead it through the pope, the bishop, and "all those who keep and cultivate the orthodox and catholic faith handed down by the apostles", that is, the legitimate pastors of the particular churches and local communities. They are the celebrated *marks* that prove the existence of communion in the Church. At the same time, the priest remembers to the Father those who are present at the celebration and make their offering: "for them we offer to you and they too offer", that is, the offering is made by the ordained priesthood and the common priesthood. In the second place, it is stated that the Mass is celebrated in communion with Mary and the saints, the heavenly Church, asking their intercession. In the third place, "the power" of God's "benediction" is invoked so that the gifts might be consecrated: the expression is referred to the Holy Spirit. Historical research has suggested that the nucleus of the Roman Canon dates to before the definition by the Council of Constantinople in 381. This should not be surprising, since another ancient Eucharistic Prayer, the Coptic anaphora of Serapion, contains an epiclesis to the Word.

Returning to the Roman Canon, after the Consecration, the priest calls to mind the Father of the Son and the Son's Paschal Mystery, offering his body and his blood as an acceptable sacrifice prefigured by those of Abel, Abraham, and Melchizedek; he pleads for the sacrifice to reach the heavenly altar from the earthly one. Then follow the intercessions for the dead, for the purification of the Church, and for the earthly Church that is celebrating in that place. The great prayer concludes with the glorification of the Trinity and the *amen* of the faithful.

From this prayer, which carefully weaves together personal and communitarian faith, emerges the communion of the Church that descends from heaven with the marks of unity, sanctity, catholicity, and apostolicity. The prayer simultaneously remembers Jesus Christ and his mystery and awaits his coming both in the liturgical present and in the final judgment. Thus the liturgy and the Church are manifested as the memory of the historical event of Christ that took place in the Holy Land two thousand years ago with the Incarnation and redemption but that is ever present in the mystery of faith and charity that is especially the Eucharist.

Therefore, the liturgy is essentially the Church's prayer of trinitarian adoration.

Now, we have said that the crisis that has shaken the liturgy often stems from the fact that men, the community, replace God as the center; thus, as J.B. Metz says: "The crisis of God is codified ecclesiologically." [1]

The disintegration of the liturgy begins when it is no longer conceived and lived as the adoration of the Trinity in Jesus Christ and as the celebration of the whole Church rather than that of a local community, a celebration of which the bishops and priests are ministers, that is, servants, and not owners. The continual lament of some liturgists about the failure to realize the reform and the expedients to make it attractive indicate that the spirit of the liturgy has been lost, that it has been reduced to the local community's celebration of itself. Doctrinal relativism hides liturgical creativity: the Eucharist is the first to have suffered from a non-Catholic idea of the Church: "I am convinced", Joseph Ratzinger writes, "that the crisis in the Church that we are experiencing today is to a large extent due to the disintegration of the liturgy." [2]

The refusal to understand the liturgical renewal from within the Catholic tradition was already manifest during the years of ecumenical gatherings. Did the new monastic communities not privilege the biblical word in the liturgy over the eucharistic celebration? Did the meal dimension of the liturgy not begin to be emphasized to the detriment of the sacrificial dimension? The Council never imagined this. Thus,

---

[1] J. Ratzinger, "The Ecclesiology of the Constitution on the Church, Vatican II, *Lumen gentium*", in *L'Osservatore Romano*, English ed., no. 38 (September 19, 2001), p. 5.

[2] J. Ratzinger, *Milestones: Memoirs: 1927–1977*, trans. E. Leiva-Merikakis (San Francisco: Ignatius Press, 1999), p. 148.

while traditionalists asked in 1982 that the doctrinal value of Vatican II be reduced, some progressivist schools have recently decided to place it among the non-ecumenical general councils of the second millennium. Who should be feared more, those who raised the specter of the *motu proprio* having "an effect similar to an atomic conflagration" or those who for decades have postulated the discontinuity and rupture between the preconciliar and the postconciliar Church? Have they not been the ones to encourage diffidence, indeed insubordination, among the people of God? Thus the traditionalists claim that the preconciliar Church was betrayed by the Council, while the progressivists claim that the postconciliar Church has betrayed the Council. To furnish an understanding of the liturgical development after the Council, in his December 22, 2005, address to the Roman curia and again in *Sacramentum caritatis*[3] Benedict XVI described such "readings" of the situation as conditioned by the hermeneutic of discontinuity or rupture.

The *motu proprio* has been called a "boorish grimace at Vatican II", but this ignores the fact that the old Roman Rite was celebrated during the Council and for a few years afterward. It is strange that those who have made John XXIII the symbol of progressivism oppose the Roman Missal that he updated and that has now been reproposed for the celebration of the old rite. The two Missals demonstrate that, beyond the different forms, the identity of the Church is unchanged. One cannot choose the Church or the Mass one pleases. Instead, all must be permitted to feel at home in the one Church participating in the old and in the new rite. This is the non-subjective criterion recalled by the *motu proprio*.

---

[3] Cf. Benedict XVI, Post-synodal Apostolic Exhortation *Sacramentum caritatis* (February 22, 2007), no. 3, n. 6.

It is foolish for those who regard themselves as prophets of the Church of the future to criticize traditionalists because they see themselves as the saviors of the Roman Church. The *motu proprio* wants both groups to be humble: the Church did not begin with Vatican II but with the apostles, and she has continued down the ages because we have received her whole in the communion of faith and love with all generations of Christians. The Church is both hierarchy and people, the image of the heavenly assembly of angels and saints, with whom she unites in the liturgy. The ecclesiology of Vatican II is the coherent result of the deepening of doctrine that has occurred across the two-millennia span of the Catholic Church's existence.

The only way to understand the *motu proprio*, then, is to situate it as a further development in continuity with the whole tradition of the Church. Those who have told the media that they do not understand the Pontiff's act but will conform in suffering obedience must open themselves to understanding the Church's history, including her most recent history, from the perspective of the continuity of the Catholic communion even in the liturgical sphere, between tradition and innovation.

The Roman Missal of Pius V, the heir of the ancient sacramentaries and the medieval missals, together with that of Paul VI is the single expression of the *lex credendi et orandi* that gives primacy to the Church's and each of her member's relationship with God.

The Missal of Pius V Was Not Abrogated

Vatican II seems to have dealt with the canonical status of the Missal of Pius V in its constitution on the liturgy: "For this reason the sacred Council, having in mind those Masses which are celebrated with the assistance of the faithful, especially on Sundays and feasts of obligation, has made the following decrees in order that the sacrifice of the Mass, even in the ritual forms of its celebration, may become pastorally efficacious to the fullest degree." [4] Here it is presumed that there are two forms of the rite of the Mass, one with the participation of the faithful, especially on Sundays and holy days of obligation (*cum populo*), and one without the assistance of the faithful (*sine populo*). It seems that the Council intended that the paragraphs of the document that followed should apply only to the rite of the Mass with the participation of the faithful. *Sacrosanctum concilium* obviously imagines that the old Mass will continue to exist as the priestly form of the celebration of the eucharistic sacrifice without the presence of the faithful; that means that the priest has the right to celebrate the old rite as a private Mass. This is all based on the following arguments:

1. The new rite of the Mass and the *General Instruction of the Roman Missal* promulgated with the apostolic constitution *Missale Romanum* of Paul VI constitute—as that document itself says—a "*renovatio*", a renewal of the Missal promulgated by Saint Pius V by decree of the Council of Trent in 1570; in fact, the constitution praises the fruits of evangelization and sanctity that followed from this Missal for four centuries.

In truth, Pius XII—the constitution observes—had already expected its recognition and enrichment, initiating a revision of the *Ordo* for Holy Week; thus, "[o]ne ought not to

---

[4] Second Vatican Council, Constitution on the Sacred Liturgy *Sacrosanctum concilium* (December 4, 1963), no. 49.

think ... that this revision of the Roman Missal has been improvident."[5] Moreover, it was renewed introducing, alongside the venerable patrimony of the Roman liturgy, new norms of celebration. The 1570 Missal itself was the result of a comparison and revision of ancient codices and liturgical sources, including Eastern ones, that had been brought to light.

2. Despite the perplexity caused by some versions in various vernaculars, the renewal of other parts of the Missal falls within the physiological process of the formation of liturgical books, beginning with the ancient Roman sacramentaries and the Eastern eucologues, which, notoriously, appeared in many versions without one abrogating another. This is the common liturgical law. The Roman Missal itself had four significant editions: the first preceding the Council of Trent in 1474; this was the one that was revised by a commission named by the Council, edited in 1570, and known as the "Missal of Pius V". It deeply influenced Catholic worship but was not exempt from modifications in the four centuries of its life. The most well-known and recent took place by order of John XXIII and was promulgated in the *editio typica* of 1962 in the wake of the reform launched by Pius XII and in reality culminated in the "Missal of Paul VI", promulgated in 1970 after the emendations we have mentioned.

If the Gregorian sacramentary and the Missal of Pius V had been abrogated, how could they have been drawn on for the *renovatio*? *Novus* simply means latest, subsequent development, and not something different, unrelated. Precisely because of this coherent progress, the Missal is the instrument of a

[5] Paul VI, Apostolic Constitution *Missale Romanum* (April 3, 1969).

certain liturgical unity in which there are "legitimate variations and adaptations".[6]

Now, everyone knows that the new rite contains no
small number of variations; indeed, these continued to
increase right up to the 2000 *editio typica*. It happens that,
on one hand, some avail themselves of this to twist,
substitute, postpone, and even omit some parts. On the
other hand, there are those who prefer to use the same
Eucharistic Prayer and the same formulas. Why should
it be surprising that some should ask to use the Roman
Canon, certain prefaces, and the ritual structure of the
1962 Roman Missal, which is inappropriately called the
"Tridentine Rite"?

So, Vatican II carried out its work in the context of the
tradition, and the legitimacy of the rite of the Mass of Paul VI
is linked to that tradition. But it cannot be opposed to the
rite of his predecessor, something that the authority of the
Church has never claimed. Thus, no liturgical book or part
of a liturgical book has been abrogated unless it contained
errors: something which, however, as we have seen, is true
of the rite published in 1969.

3. Everyone is asked to recognize an eloquent expression
of the tradition of the Church in the Missal. It does not
make sense to delegitimize anything in the old rite—it would
be like cutting away one's own roots—from which the new
one comes, which in its turn manifests the fecundity of the
old one. John Paul II noted that "in the Roman Missal of
Saint Pius V, as in several Eastern liturgies, there are very
beautiful prayers through which the priest expresses the most
profound sense of humility and reverence before the Sacred

---

[6] Cf. *Sacrosanctum concilium*, nos. 38–40.

Mysteries: they reveal the very substance of the Liturgy."[7] It need not be said, moreover, that the criterion of mutual generosity and mercy should prevail in the Church in imitation of the Lord. This, precisely, is the meaning of the indult to celebrate the Mass according to the 1962 Roman Missal that John Paul II granted on October 3, 1984, and now the meaning of Benedict XVI's *motu proprio*; the liturgical movement itself is not discredited, but the concern for the Church's unity prevails.[8] Against every kind of rigidity with respect to the liturgy, the principle *Ecclesia semper reformanda*, measured by the Gospel dictum about the new and the old (*nova et vetera*), must hold.

These arguments denying the abrogation of the Missal of Pius V only supplement the letter to the bishops that accompanied the *motu proprio*. Cardinal Newman said that the Church never abolished or prohibited orthodox forms of the liturgy because that would be foreign to the spirit of the Church (see *Parochial and Plain Sermons*, bk. 2, sermon 7). Vatican II ordered a reform of the liturgical books, but it did not prohibit the previous ones. Is it not a contradiction to welcome our Orthodox brethren into our churches with their ancient rites and chase out the Catholics who desire to celebrate the Roman Mass in the old form?

All of this must be evaluated in light of the criteria indicated in the Constitution on the Liturgy.[9] Certainly, the old liturgy suffered a little because of the individualism and

---

[7] John Paul II, "Lettera alla Plenaria della Congregazione per il Culto Divino" (September 21, 2001); English translation from *Adoremus Bulletin*, online edition, vol. 7, no. 9 (December 2001–January 2002): http://www.adoremus.org/1201-0102PopeJPIILitAssemb.html (accessed December 13, 2011).

[8] Cf. O. Nußbaum, "Die bedingte Wiederzulassung einer Meßfeier nach dem Missale Romanum von 1962", *Pastoralblatt* 37 (1985): 130–43.

[9] *Sacrosanctum concilium*, nos. 34–36.

privatism that insinuated themselves into it and made the communion between the priest and the people insufficient. Nevertheless, looking at the relationship between the old and the new rite, it is worthwhile to bear in mind the words of Paul VI: "This promulgation does not in truth change the traditional doctrine. What Christ wants, we also want. What was, remains. What the Church taught for centuries, we likewise teach." [10] Despite this, there were those who, on the occasion of the promulgation of the *motu proprio*, wrote that the introductory document, namely, the Pope's letter to the bishops, was too concise a historical summary and suggested that, for the first time, we will have two forms of the same Roman Rite.

It was also observed that with the two forms unity would be lost for the sake of a privatistic spirituality without communal relationships and that this would cause many problems. But many historical particulars were overlooked. For example, there is the fact that Annibale Bugnini, whom Paul VI put in charge of the postconciliar reform, wanted to obtain an explicit decree that the new rite of 1970 would abrogate the old Mass in such a way that the latter would be legally suppressed.

To request this decree formally from the pontifical commission for the interpretation of the conciliar documents, he needed the permission of the cardinal secretary of state. The secretary of state refused this permission on the grounds that it would constitute persistent hatred of the liturgical tradition.[11] After this fruitless endeavor, the Congregation for Divine Worship published the document *Conferentiarum*

---

[10] Paul VI, speech, November 21, 1964.

[11] Cf. A. Bugnini, *The Reform of the Liturgy: 1948–1975*, trans. M.J. O'Connell (Collegeville, Minn.: Liturgical Press, 1990), pp. 300–301.

episcopalium, to which many refer in claiming the suppression of the 1962 Missal and contesting the Pope's statement in the *motu proprio* that there was never such a suppression. That document indeed claims that only the new Missal is permitted, while the old one is not, except for *Missa sine populo* and old and infirm priests. According to some, the later law abrogates the previous one. And yet, canon 21 of the Code of Canon Law states: "In a case of doubt the revocation of a pre-existent law is not presumed, but later laws are to be related to earlier ones and, insofar as it is possible, harmonized with them." Thus the document of the Congregation for Divine Worship, *Conferentiarum episcopalium*, clearly goes farther than is permissible in prohibiting the 1962 Missal.

But there is another decisive historical detail to support the view that the old Missal was not abrogated. In 1986, Pope John Paul II instituted a commission of nine cardinals to examine the juridical status of the 1962 Missal. Cardinals Casaroli, Gantin, Mayer, Innocenti, Oddi, Palazzini, Ratzinger, Stickler, and Tomko were the ones John Paul II appointed, and they had the task of verifying whether the new rite of the Mass promulgated by Paul VI abrogated the old Mass and whether a bishop could prohibit his priests from celebrating it.

The commission met in December 1986. Eight out of the nine cardinals responded to the first question by saying that the new Mass had not abrogated the old one. All nine affirmed that Paul VI had never given the bishops authority to prohibit priests from celebrating the Mass according to the Missal of Saint Pius V. The commission then judged that the conditions of the 1984 indult were too restrictive and proposed that they be loosened. These conclusions served as operative guidelines for the *Ecclesia Dei* Commission but were never promulgated.

Nevertheless, in this connection, it has been observed that the Holy See recognized the right of priests to celebrate the traditional Mass; this stemmed from the fact that if any priest was suspended for having celebrated the old Mass against the bishop's will, the sanction was always nullified by the Roman Curia if an appeal was made. So, the famous meeting of the cardinals had been decisive.

There are those who mention the following statement of Paul VI: "The new *Ordo* has been promulgated to replace the old."[12] The liturgical reform involved renewed liturgical books. Therefore the Pope, as was right, put his trust in a collaborator, at least until a certain moment. When he realized that corrections had to be made to the new *Ordo*, the utmost was done, but that did not stop him from proceeding. It was not strange that rites and texts were revised when doctrinal and other issues were noted. Liturgical books—like any ecclesiastical institution—are not irreformable. After all, does not the new Missal retrieve ancient texts and rites that had fallen into disuse? An indult, thus, presupposes the existence of a norm that has been abandoned, in our case, one that has prohibited but not abolished the old Mass. Therefore, John Paul II reestablished it. The indult serves to remove a prohibition, to revoke an abrogation wherever it has occurred. In regard to the abolition—a term that in Latin means suppression or destruction—of the Missal of Pius V, it is obviously unimaginable. How can the innovative liturgists claim an abrogation when at the same time they say that Vatican II did not intend to create a new rite? Do they hold that Vatican II is more restrictive than Trent? And how much do they respect the freedom of priests and the faithful? Is creativity to be tolerated but not fidelity to tradition?

[12] Consistory Speech, May 24, 1976.

Finally, the third *editio typica* of the Roman Missal does not contain any clause that abrogates the old form of the Roman Rite. So, where are the proofs for an abrogation? The *motu proprio*, then, did not cause any confusion but, rather, rests on a solid theological basis.

Cardinal Ratzinger noted that "rites can disappear if those who follow them during a certain period disappear or if their conditions of life change. The authority of the Church has the power to define and limit the use of certain rites in different historical situations, but it cannot prohibit them purely and simply! Thus the Council prepared the reform of the liturgical books, but it did not prohibit the previous books." [13] Elsewhere, on the same topic, he noted that, "[f]or fostering a true consciousness in liturgical matters, it is also important that the proscription against the form of the liturgy in valid use up to 1970 should be lifted. Anyone who nowadays advocates the continuing existence of this liturgy or takes part in it is treated like a leper; all tolerance ends here. There has never been anything like this in history; in doing this we are despising and proscribing the Church's whole past. How can one trust her present if things are that way? I must say, quite openly, that I don't understand why so many of my episcopal brethren have to a great extent submitted to this rule of intolerance, which for no apparent reason is opposed to making the necessary inner reconciliations within the Church." [14]

The rigidity and uniformity displayed by some against *Summorum pontificum*—the same ones who are champions of liturgical variety—have never been the practice of the

---

[13] Address for the tenth anniversary of the John Paul II's *motu proprio Ecclesia Dei*, Rome, October 24, 1998.

[14] J. Ratzinger, *God and the World: A Conversation with Peter Seewald*, trans. H. Taylor (San Francisco: Ignatius Press, 2002), p. 416.

Church. John Paul II's indult had already been an invitation to tolerance.

So, let us return to our question: Can it be said that the different liturgical books convey different ideas of the Church? Can there be different styles of celebrating? There certainly are different styles of celebrating, but it is not the fault of the new rite; rather, it is on account of widespread abuses. To claim that the two Missals offer very different ecclesiological, theological, and liturgical paradigms, opposing the Church as communion and people of God[15] to the Church as hierarchical society of the Council of Trent, is doctrinally erroneous insofar as Vatican II itself says that the Church is "constituted and organized in the world as a society" [16] and has a "hierarchical structure" (cf. the title of *Lumen gentium*'s third chapter).

Furthermore, if it is true that the ancient Gelasian and Leonine patrimony was introduced into the Missal of Paul VI, why must the Gregorian patrimony in the Tridentine Missal be abandoned? In fact, scholars such as Lauren Pristas have undermined the thesis that the liturgical reform drew from ancient sources: she has shown that the majority of the prayers have been constructed *ex novo*, replacing those of the most ancient liturgical books.[17] It would be helpful if her studies were known in Italy.

With the *motu proprio*, those who use the old liturgical books—even on a daily basis—always do so in an extraordinary way with respect to the whole Church, which uses the ordinary books; as also every priest is called to celebrate the

---

[15] Second Vatican Council, Dogmatic Council on the Church *Lumen gentium* (November 21, 1964), nos. 1–2.

[16] Ibid., no. 8.

[17] For example: "The Orations of the Vatican II Missal: Policies for Revision", *Communio* 30 (2003): 621–53.

extraordinary form even if he celebrates the ordinary form daily. The liberalization of the Missal of Pius V does not nullify Vatican II's constitution on the liturgy, but it does relativize certain instructions about the constitution's application, which often infringed on the principles of the old Missal. Did the Council envision Mass celebrated *facing the people* or the total abolition of Latin and Gregorian chant? We are all more humble, understanding, tolerant, and ecumenical internally since we are externally with non-Catholics, non-Christians, and non-believers. There is no such thing as a "spirit of the liturgy" for the man of today after Vatican II. The spirit is always the same: bless and adore God; the forms of this are various exteriorly and interiorly, from East to West.

Now is the moment for a deeper understanding of the liturgy, for the maturation of the faith, for a feeling for the universal Church.

Two Theories Originating from Biblicism

It is maintained that the postconciliar liturgy is richer in readings, in Eucharistic Prayers, while the Missal of Pius V is poorer, less thorough. It is an anachronistic thesis because it does not take into account the distance of four centuries; it would be similar to criticizing the sacramentaries that existed before Pius V's for the same thing. Furthermore, it is forgotten that the pericopes of this Missal were formed on the basis of the ancient capitularies with epistles, such as the *Liber comitis* of Saint Jerome—dating from 471—or the Gospel pericopes, a tradition that is common to the East, as we still see in the Byzantine liturgy today. In the second place, the brief readings help one to memorize the essential and express the sobriety of the Roman Rite.

It is claimed that the old rite does not emphasize Christ's presence in the word when this is proclaimed in the assembly; thus the essence itself of the liturgical action is diminished, an action that is constituted by the *two tables*[18] that form a single act of worship! The Missal of the Council of Trent is alleged to work from a perspective that is far from the tradition of the Fathers of the Church; it is regarded as a missal that was born exclusively for the priest and does not foresee the participation of the assembly because, supposedly, it does not understand the people as an integral part of the liturgy. In reality, the priest is celebrating for himself *and* the people. But it is further suggested—by those who see the Missal of Paul VI as superior to that of Pius V— that the former, unlike the latter, does not conceive the priest as the celebrant but the Church, sacramentally present in the assembly, of whom the priest, by the power of his ordination, is the natural president.

It is a mentality that, in a Protestant way, reduces everything to word and assembly. "Jesus is not just the teacher, but also the Redeemer of the whole person. The Jesus who teaches is at the same time the Jesus who saves" [19]—and it is only through the eucharistic Sacrament that this efficaciously happens.

Another theory that is in circulation, because of the typical phenomenon of substituting one thing for another, is making Jesus Christ's presence in the Blessed Sacrament equal with his presence in the word of the book of the Scriptures. Now, Jesus is present in this word only "when the holy scriptures

---

[18] In Second Vatican Council, Dogmatic Constitution on Divine Revelation *Dei Verbum* (November 18, 1965), no. 21, there seems to be just *one*.

[19] J. Ratzinger, *Jesus of Nazareth: From the Baptism in the Jordan to the Transfiguration*, trans. A. Walker (New York et al.: Doubleday, 2008), p. 65.

are read in the Church".[20] Therefore, there are two conditions for Christ's presence in the word: the reading must occur *in church*, not privately, and the Sacred Scriptures must be *read*, the mere fact of the book's being on the ambo or on the altar is not sufficient. Christ's presence in the world is transitory, linked to use, a moral presence, while the presence in the eucharistic Sacrament is substantial and permanent, not dependent on the celebration. Furthermore, the presence of God in the word is mediated, linked to an act of the spirit, to the spiritual condition of the individual, and limited in time.

The consequence of this equivocation is evident in many parts of the world: the claim, or the insinuation, that the real presence in the Eucharist is linked to *use* and ends with it, that it is a question of degree and not of substance.

Thus, it is especially important to reaffirm the inescapable—and at the same time asymmetrical—connection between the word and the Eucharist as stated by *Dei Verbum*, no. 21: "The Church has always venerated the divine Scriptures just as (*sicut*) she venerates the body of the Lord." How is this to be understood? The Pontifical Commission for the Interpretation of the Decrees of Vatican Council II explains it thus: "In these words the adverb *sicut* does not imply that the Sacred Scriptures are owed a veneration that is the same, that is, equal, to that of the Most Holy Eucharist. One must venerate both the Sacred Scriptures and the Body of the Lord, but in a different way and aspect, as is inferred by the constitution on the sacred liturgy *Sacrosanctum Concilium*, no. 7, by the encyclical *Mysterium fidei* of September 3, 1965, in nos. 17–20, and by the instruction *Eucharisticum Mysterium*, no. 9."[21]

---

[20] *Sacrosanctum concilium*, no. 7.

[21] Cf. *Responso*, February 5, 1968, *Acta Apostolicae Sedis* 60 (Rome: Typis Polyglottis Vaticanis, 1968), p. 362.

It is more necessary than ever that preaching and catechesis return to stressing again the proper distinction between
revelation, the word of God, and Sacred Scripture, which,
though intimately connected, are not equivalent. Sometimes, in fact, in this respect one surprisingly meets significant confusion, and not only among the lay faithful. We
have indeed come to the point where it is claimed that the
Bible is interpreted by the Bible, and not in the tradition
and with the help of the Magisterium.

VI

HOW TO ENCOUNTER THE MYSTERY

The Priestly Service

The liturgical writings of Joseph Ratzinger the theologian and cardinal—like his interventions as Pope—are seen by some liturgists as the trespassing of a poacher on their hunting ground, subtly implying his incompetence in the field as if the liturgy had nothing to do with dogma and theology except when they want to invoke the axiom *lex orandi/lex credendi* to support their own theses. The truth is that the Holy Father always leads reflection on the liturgy back to the question of whether it is not essentially worship of God. He begins by asking: "What precisely *is* worship?" [1] It is the giving of everything to God, all of history and the cosmos, beginning with ourselves: this is the essence of worship and of "sacrifice". It is cosmic liturgy because it integrates creation and redemption, in the sense of the celebrated study by Hans Urs von Balthasar on Saint Maximus the Confessor. [2]

[1] J. Ratzinger, *The Spirit of the Liturgy*, trans. J. Saward (San Francisco: Ignatius Press, 2000), p. 27.

[2] Hans Urs von Balthasar, *Cosmic Liturgy: The Universe according to Maximus the Confessor*, trans. B. E. Daley (San Francisco: Ignatius Press, 2003).

Many have lost a sense for the liturgy because they have lost a sense of the divine presence in our midst: that which, according to legend, stupefied the envoys of Prince Vladimir of Kiev in the Basilica of Hagia Sophia in Constantinople in 987; sent to determine which form of worship to adopt, they were in awe, not knowing whether they were in heaven or on earth, before the indescribable splendor of the Byzantine liturgy: "We know only that the Lord visits these men and that their service is the most luminous of all nations."

Could the same be said of our liturgies today? Are they the place where the God of heaven and earth dwells and lives, as the patriarch Saint Germanus of Constantinople said? One must be honest: even in Latin liturgies, an encounter with the mystery cannot take place in a void but only in a unitary system of ritual symbolism, organized space and images, and interpretation of the faith;[3] otherwise everything becomes ambiguous and enigmatic.

"Man can never be redeemed simply from outside":[4] Benedict XVI's criticism of a Christianity that has let itself be permeated by the influence of modernity, and by rationalism in particular, can be applied to the liturgy, and it reveals that rationalism has reduced its value. In the present situation, the liturgy is not just a ritual question: knowing what the rite means formally and symbolically is insufficient if it is not understood as the sign of the faith of the participants, of the elevation of the mind to God "so that they may offer Him rational service and more abundantly

---

[3] In regard to the Byzantine Eucharist, see the important study of H.-J. Schultz, *The Byzantine Liturgy: Symbolic Structure and Faith Expression* (New York: Pueblo, 1986).

[4] Benedict XVI, Encyclical *Spe salvi* (November 30, 2007), no. 25.

receive His grace".[5] Too much importance has been placed on the later effects of the rite, on what happens afterward. The efficaciousness is immediate: it is less in our speaking and more in a communication to our being. The rite permits God to be inexpressible, unspeakable: it is better to contemplate the mystery than to conceptualize it. This is the reason for the minster's and the faithful's unconditional obedience to the rite. The Holy Mass is like a piece of music written by a composer: it must be executed with fidelity.

In chapter 5 of *Jesus of Nazareth*, which is dedicated to the Lord's Prayer, the Pope recalls how the Lord himself warned against erroneous forms of prayer and two in particular: self-exhibition in place of adoration and excess of words that choke the Spirit. If prayer is the expression of love between an individual and God, it contains a mystery that does not tolerate spectacle to "be seen by men" (Mt 6:5). In times characterized by the mania of appearances, this temptation can touch the priests who celebrate the liturgy, especially those who direct it like a "master of ceremonies", betraying at times the exaggerated, if not perverse, tendency to put oneself on display, what we call exhibitionism. Perhaps it is an effect of standing up in front of the assembly instead of being turned toward the Lord, before whom even the communal dimension, evidenced by the plural *noster* of the *Pater noster*, "awakens the inmost core of the person".[6] This is true for every human being, for every Christian; nevertheless, the priest is called to express his personal relation and that of the community with God: "The 'we' of the praying community and the utterly

---

[5] Second Vatican Council, Constitution on the Sacred Liturgy *Sacrosanctum concilium* (December 4, 1963), no. 33.

[6] J. Ratzinger, *Jesus of Nazareth: From the Baptism in the Jordan to the Transfiguration*, trans. A. Walker (New York et al.: Doubleday, 2008), p. 129.

personal intimacy that can be shared only with God are closely
interconnected." [7]

The priest is a bridge to establish relations between God
and men. He must therefore be aware of the mystery with
which he comes into contact and express it above all with
humble prayer. He knows that by means of the eucharistic
celebration he participates in the mystery "that . . . was from
the beginning" (1 Jn 1:1). Benedict XVI so effectively out-
lines this priestly service in a 2008 homily for the Chrism
Mass in Saint Peter's Basilica that we would like to quote
his remarks at length:

> What does this "being a priest of Jesus Christ" mean? The
> Second Canon of our Missal, which was probably com-
> piled in Rome already at the end of the second century,
> describes the essence of the priestly ministry with the words
> with which, in the Book of Deuteronomy (18:5, 7), the
> essence of the Old Testament priesthood is described: *astare
> coram te et tibi ministrare* ["to stand and minister in the name
> of the Lord"]. There are therefore two duties that define
> the essence of the priestly ministry: in the first place, "to
> stand in his [the Lord's] presence". . . . Now if this word is
> found in the Canon of the Mass immediately after the con-
> secration of the gifts, after the entrance of the Lord in the
> assembly of prayer, then for us this points to being before
> the Lord present, that is, it indicates the Eucharist as the
> center of priestly life. . . .
>
> Now let us move on to the second word that the Sec-
> ond Canon repeats from the Old Testament text—"to stand
> in your presence and serve you". The priest must be an
> upright person, vigilant, a person who remains standing.
> Service is then added to all this. In the Old Testament

text this word has an essentially ritualistic meaning: all acts of worship foreseen by the Law are the priests' duty. But this action, according to the rite, was classified as service, as a duty of service, and thus it explains in what spirit this activity must take place. With the assumption of the word "serve" in the Canon, the liturgical meaning of this term was adopted in a certain way—to conform with the novelty of the Christian cult. What the priest does at that moment, in the Eucharistic celebration, is to serve, to fulfill a service to God and a service to humanity. The cult that Christ rendered to the Father was the giving of himself to the end for humanity. Into this cult, this service, the priest must insert himself. Thus, the word "serve" contains many dimensions. In the first place, part of it is certainly the correct celebration of the liturgy and of the sacraments in general, accomplished through interior participation. We must learn to increasingly understand the sacred liturgy in all its essence, to develop a living familiarity with it, so that it becomes the soul of our daily life. It is then that we celebrate in the correct way; it is then that the *ars celebrandi*, the art of celebrating, emerges by itself. In this art there must be nothing artificial. If the liturgy is the central duty of the priest, this also means that prayer must be a primary reality, to be learned ever anew and ever more deeply at the school of Christ and of the Saints of all the ages. Since the Christian liturgy by its nature is also always a proclamation, we must be people who are familiar with the Word of God, love it and live by it: only then can we explain it in an adequate way. "To serve the Lord"—priestly service precisely also means to learn to know the Lord in his Word and to make it known to all those he entrusts to us.

Lastly, two other aspects are part of service. No one is closer to his master than the servant who has access to the most private dimensions of his life. In this sense "to serve" means closeness, it requires familiarity. This familiarity also bears a danger: when we continually encounter the sacred it risks becoming habitual for us. In this way, reverential fear is extinguished. Conditioned by all our habits we no longer perceive the great, new and surprising fact that he himself is present, speaks to us, gives himself to us. We must ceaselessly struggle against this becoming accustomed to the extraordinary reality, against the indifference of the heart, always recognizing our insufficiency anew and the grace that there is in the fact that he consigned himself into our hands. To serve means to draw near, but above all it also means obedience. The servant is under the word: "not my will, but thine, be done" (Lk 22:42).... Our obedience is a believing with the Church, a thinking and speaking with the Church, serving through her. What Jesus predicted to Peter also always applies: "You will be taken where you do not want to go." This letting oneself be guided where one does not want to be led is an essential dimension of our service, and it is exactly what makes us free. In this being guided, which can be contrary to our ideas and plans, we experience something new—the wealth of God's love.

The Holy Father's words constitute an admirable counterpoint to what is said in a summary way in the 1969 *General Instruction of the Roman Missal*:

A priest . . . , who possesses within the Church the power of Holy Orders to offer sacrifice in the person of Christ, stands for this reason at the head of the faithful people gathered together here and now, presides over their prayer, proclaims the message of salvation to them, associates the people with himself in the offering of sacrifice through Christ in the Holy Spirit to God the Father, gives his brothers and sisters the Bread of eternal life, and partakes of it with them. When he celebrates the Eucharist, therefore, *he must serve God and the people with dignity and humility*, and by his bearing and by the way he says the divine words he must convey to the faithful the living presence of Christ.[8]

The Participation of the Faithful

Saint Cyprian, Bishop of Carthage in the third century, recommends that those who pray should do so in silence and fear, thinking themselves to be in God's sight, and observes: "We must please the divine eyes both with the habit of body and with the measure of voice. For as it is characteristic of a shameless man to be noisy with his cries, so, on the other hand, it is fitting to the modest man to pray with moderated petitions." That is Cyprian's recommendation when one prays in private. About public prayer he advises the following:

> When we meet together with the brethren ... and celebrate divine sacrifices with God's priest, we ought to be mindful of modesty and discipline—not to throw abroad our prayers indiscriminately, with unsubdued voices, nor to cast to God a petition that ought to be commended to God by modesty; for God is the hearer, not of the voice, but of the heart. Nor need He be clamorously reminded, since He sees men's thoughts.... The Holy Spirit, moreover, suggests these same things by Jeremiah, and teaches, saying, "But in the heart ought God to be adored by thee" (Bar 6:6). And let not the worshipper, beloved brethren, be ignorant in what manner the publican prayed with the Pharisee in the temple. Not with eyes lifted up boldly to heaven, nor with hands proudly raised; but beating his breast, and

[8] *General Instruction of the Roman Missal, editio typica latina*, no. 60; *editio typica tertia*, III, no. 93 (italics added).

testifying to the sins shut up within, he implored the help of the divine mercy.[9]

Cyprian concludes that this is the "right way" to pray, which obtains God's justification and salvation.

Maximus the Confessor observes that Christ makes man a participant in God's salvific action. Does not participation in the liturgy aim at renewing this cooperation?

Rivers of ink have been spilled on participation in the liturgy. How many have written that before the Council the liturgy did not favor participation and that with the Council the liturgy has been restored to the people! When certain liturgists want to defend their idea or taste, they say: the people must participate. It is a neo-clericalism that has infected even the laity. Participation has been mistakenly presented as a discovery of the Council. There exists in the Roman liturgy the concept of *facti participes*, that is, our being "made to participate" in an action that is not our own, even if it is accomplished in a human discourse, because God became word and then flesh: "The real 'action' in the liturgy", Ratzinger could write, "in which we are all supposed to participate is the action of God himself. That is what is new and distinctive about the Christian liturgy: God himself acts and does what is essential." [10] If we are not aware of being made participants, the "attitudes" that are to be assumed in the liturgy become a form of aestheticism. This is the reason why the principal attitude of adoration—which unites, among others, Catholics and

[9] Cyprian, Treatise IV, "On the Lord's Prayer", nos. 4–6, trans. Ernest Wallis, in *Ante-Nicene Fathers*, vol. 5: *Hippolytus, Cyprian, Caius, Novatian, Appendix*, ed. Alexander Roberts and James Donaldson, rev. A. Cleveland Coxe (Peabody, Mass.: Hendrickson Publishers, 1995), 448–49; *Corpus Scriptorum Ecclesiasticorum Latinorum*, 3:268–70.

[10] Ratzinger, *Spirit of the Liturgy*, p. 173.

Orthodox but also Jews and Muslims—prostration or kneeling, has almost been forbidden: some spiritual directors have
even gone so far as to prohibit seminarians from kneeling
because this is allegedly an indicator of devotionalism or an
inauthentic vocation. It is strange that so many liturgists
who are so attentive to claiming the primacy of Scripture
have failed to acknowledge its emphasis on kneeling. Ratzinger draws our attention to this: "The central importance
of kneeling in the Bible can be seen in a very concrete way.
The word *proskynein* alone occurs fifty-nine times in the
New Testament, twenty-four of which are in the Apoca-
lypse, the book of the heavenly liturgy, which is presented
to the Church as the standard for her own liturgy." [11] And
so it is. If the Christian liturgy is not before all else the
public and integral worship, the adoration, of God, the Apoc-
alypse cannot be the *typikon*, the normative book. From
where else would the various liturgical books have drawn
their cogent force? What the liturgy affirms and asks to be
observed is a divine law, not a human one: "The Christian
liturgy is a cosmic liturgy precisely because it bends the
knee before the crucified and exalted Lord. Here is the center of authentic culture—the culture of truth. The humble
gesture by which we fall at the feet of the Lord inserts us
into the true path of the life of the cosmos." [12] We have
chosen this gesture from among all others; it is the most
important one, the one that sums up the spirit of the liturgy.

Despite the extraordinary pages on the devotion proper
to each member of the body of Christ written by Saint
Francis de Sales, after the Council a division was created
between participation and devotion. And yet in *Mediator*

[11] Ibid., pp. 185–86.
[12] Ibid., p. 193.

Dei Pius XII points out how the piety of the people nota-
bly contributed to the development of the liturgy. In the
1967 instruction of the Sacred Congregation of Rites *Eucharisticum mysterium*, a central truth expounded by Saint Thomas
is recalled: "Like the passion of Christ itself, this sacrifice,
though offered for all, 'has no effect except in those united
to the passion of Christ by faith and charity.... To these it
brings a greater or less benefit in proportion to their devotion.' " [13] Catholic worship, however, has gone from adoration of God to the exhibition of the priest, the ministers,
and the faithful. Piety has been abolished as a word and
liquidated by liturgists as devotionalism, but they have made
the people, placing too much emphasis on them, put up
with liturgical experiments and rejected spontaneous forms
of devotion and piety. They have even succeeded in imposing applause on funerals in place of mourning and weep-
ing. Did Christ not mourn and weep at the death of Lazarus?
Ratzinger rightly observes: "Wherever applause breaks out
in the liturgy because of some human achievement, it is a
sure sign that the essence of the liturgy has totally disappeared and been replaced by a kind of religious entertain-
ment." [14] Is there any bishop who has the courage to go
against the current?

Looking upon the Cross

Until the Council, all Christians of the East and the West,
including priests, prayed toward the apse, which, at least

---

[13] Saint Thomas Aquinas, *Summa theologiae*, III, q. 79, a. 7 ad 2, cited in
Sacred Congregation of Rites, Instruction on Eucharistic Worship *Mysterium
Eucharisticum* (May 25, 1967), no. 12.

[14] Ratzinger, *Spirit of the Liturgy*, p. 198.

until the sixteenth century, faced east. In Western churches, as in those of the East, prominent in the apse were the cross, a painting of one of the Christian mysteries or the saint for whom the church was named, and the altar with the tabernacle. The priest and the faithful did not doubt that in praying they both needed to face the same direction. The priest turned to the faithful only for exhortations, readings, and the homily. All Christians celebrated in this way from the first centuries. Jungmann, the celebrated Innsbruck liturgist, who participated in the Council, opposed the slogan according to which in the past the priest "turned his back" on the faithful and insisted that both were "turned toward the Lord".

Today there are those who claim that what counts is not so much the exterior orientation as the interior attitude taken by the faithful before the mystery that is celebrated. But the liturgy speaks with external signs; otherwise it falls into contradiction. Precisely because the liturgy speaks through symbols, Ratzinger does not fail to observe that at its foundation is the cosmic and allegorical conception of the commentators and Fathers, from Theodore of Mopsuestia to Maximus the Confessor, and to suggest that, "wherever possible, we should definitely take up again the apostolic tradition of facing the east, both in the building of churches and in the celebration of the liturgy." [15] At least new church buildings could be constructed with this advice in mind.

The most conspicuous move in the postconciliar liturgical reform has been the change in the priest's position toward the people to give the idea of a community that participates in the *Lord's supper*: but, because of the way in which it is carried out, it resembles, if anything, a snack. Now

[15] Ibid., p. 70.

who would propose turning an orchestra conductor around to face the public? Looking at how priests in the Eastern Churches celebrate, one becomes aware, in fact, of having abandoned in the new rite the apostolic tradition, from which, Saint Basil says, we have received the instruction to "face east during prayer.... We all look together toward the east as we pray; but few know that we seek the ancient homeland, the paradise that God planted in Eden, in the east." [16]

The liturgical movement of the early twentieth century supported the celebration of the Mass *versus populum* and began to adapt the altar. Nevertheless, the Council did not accept this practice. A subsequent instruction proposed that the altar be placed in such a way as to permit the second part of the Mass to be celebrated "facing the people" and no longer facing east; nevertheless, it was not an obligation but a possibility. The Congregation for Divine Worship later confirmed that celebrating facing the people was not obligatory.[17]

The eastward direction of prayer was already established in Christian antiquity in relation to the cross, understood as the "interior east of faith". Thus, the cross is at the center of the altar as an image and not as an accessory. Why must this be seen as a visual obstacle between the celebrant and the faithful? What could be better in the liturgy than everyone turning toward the cross and the image of the Crucified upon it? From the moment it is enthroned, as in the old rite of Good Friday, it must always be venerated. It is there to remind us that Christ's sacrifice is the *form* of the

---

[16] Saint Basil, *De Spiritu sancto*, chap. 27, no. 66.

[17] Cf. *Responsum ad dubium*, September 25, 2000. On the topic of orientation in general, see U. M. Lang, *Turning Towards the Lord*, 2nd ed. (San Francisco: Ignatius Press, 2009).

Eucharist. The cross is a precondition for celebrating the liturgy facing the people, for it is a reminder of the fundamental attitude of prayer: *conversi ad Dominum*, turned—and converted—to the Lord.[18]

At the beginning of the reform, there was no discussion about the cross on the altar or suspended above it in a way that allowed the gaze of both the priest and the people to rest upon it. Then the theory began to be floated that it could be moved, and it finally ended up behind the priest—often along with the tabernacle—no longer the object of attention; this happened while certain orientaphiles were multiplying icons at the side of the altar in hopes they would receive more veneration. This indicates that it is still felt to be necessary to aid the faithful through images.

Then, the contemporary celebration puts the priest at the center with his chair: it has become a liturgy *versus presbyterum* and no longer one *versus Deum*! The priest has become more important than the cross, the altar, and the tabernacle! Let us learn from the Eastern liturgy and from the old Mass (regarded as "clerical") in which the bishop's *cathedra* and the celebrant's chair are to the right and to the left of the altar, situated in such a way that they do not turn their backs on the altar and are able to look upon it and the cross—which are together the great sign of Christ—and at the same time be at the head of the assembly of the faithful.

It would not take much work to return things to this configuration. The cross, in particular, must be moved back to the center of the altar or above it, as Benedict XVI has started to do in the celebrations over which he presides.

---

[18] Cf. J. Ratzinger, *The Feast of Faith: Approaches to a Theology of the Liturgy*, trans. G. Harrison (San Francisco: Ignatius Press, 1986), p. 145.

Only Christ can be at the center of our attention (cf. Lk 4:21) if the signs are to mean anything!

The sacred liturgy requires our humility. "We humbly pray to you." Humility is the true measure of the liturgy, and consequently the true measure of ourselves, because we are creatures and in need of everything. Thus understood, humility is truth. Is not true worship that which is carried out in spirit and in truth? And it is toward the truth that the intellect is directed. The priest's mediation between God and the people is not his moment for self-actualization; rather he must submit himself to the mediation performed by Jesus Christ. Thus the priest must be aware that he cannot put himself, and much less his opinions, but only Christ in first place. The true meaning of *pròestos*—which is not captured by the word "president"—is to *stand before the others* and, in this way, *praesedens*. From the Syrian *Didascalia* we know that the bishop stood in front of or at the head of the community that looked upon the altar facing east. It also directs the bishop, should a poor man enter the assembly, to cede his place to him, something he could not do were he seated in front on a throne. Once again, this means *humility*.[19]

The Sacrality of the Church Building

In 1948 the Austrian art historian Hans Sedlmayr published *Verlust der Mitte: Die bildende Kunst des 19. und 20. Jahrhunderts als Symptom und Symbol der Zeit.*[20] The book is a diagnosis that identifies the cause of the malady of Western

---

[19] Cf. Benedict XVI, Post-synodal Apostolic Exhortation *Sacramentum caritatis* (February 22, 2007), no. 23.

[20] Hans Sedlmayr, *Art in Crisis: The Lost Center*, trans. B. Battershaw (New Brunswick, N.J.: Transaction Publishers, 2007).

architecture and art as the separation of the divine and the human to the detriment of the latter. There is an analogous crisis of unity in the figurative arts, architecture, painting, and sculpture, that go into church construction. For centuries these arts worked harmoniously together in the creation of Christian churches. Now they all go off in their own directions. Today the ecclesiastical customer tends generally to ask the architect to create the space and then, separately, the painter and the sculptor (if there is time and money left) to take care of the decorative work.

The loss of the center must be understood first of all in a spiritual sense: we need to bring back to the center of Christian art its primary cause, namely, the presence of the mystery that the artist makes visible. The debate about the means, the forms, and the styles in which this mystery is expressed must have this as its guide.

In our day Christoph Cardinal Schönborn asks why so much sacred art is so ugly (including, in his view, the modern collection in the Vatican Museums) and, in the second place, why the liturgy has lost a sense of the beautiful. The answer he himself furnishes is that it is a consequence of the loss of a sense of the sacred, that is, of the ability to perceive the mystery of God's presence.[21] The pictorial image of the divine presence—the icon of Eastern Christianity—is quasi-sacramental.

Joseph Ratzinger has dealt with the question of images in the liturgy, recalling the central place of the Incarnation: "this descent of God" occurred and occurs "to draw us into a movement of ascent. . . . The Incarnation is rightly understood only when it is seen within the broad context

---

[21] C. Schönborn, *A Sua immagine e somiglianza* (Torino: Edizioni Lindau, 2008).

of creation, history, and the new world."[22] What should
be said of a certain spiritualism that is in vogue today that
mortifies the senses, that condemns the Apostle Thomas,
who wanted to believe through sight? Jesus thus made himself visible to Thomas—and to the other apostles (otherwise, why did the Word become man?). It is not as if with
the Resurrection God changed his method. As Leo the Great
said, the Lord's visibility passed into the sacraments. Thomas
was reproved for not having believed in the beginning of
the apostolic tradition; he did not believe in what they had
seen: the other apostles had seen, touched, and eaten with
the Lord eight days earlier, and they had reported this to
Thomas, who was absent. This is why Jesus says "Blessed
are those who, though they have not seen, have believed."
Believed in what? They have believed in that which others
before them saw first and handed down to them. This is
the *apostolic tradition* of which the liturgy is an integral part:
some famous "liturgical" documents of Christian antiquity
have this very title.

The liturgy itself would not make sense without the senses.
Thus, Ratzinger stresses that "the senses are not to be dis-
carded, but they should be expanded to their widest capacity." Ratzinger does not say this because he fails to recognize
God's transcendence. Referencing a distinction proposed by
Gregory Palamas and Paul Evdokimov, he continues: "In
his essence God is radically transcendent, but in his existence he can be, and wants to be, represented as the Living
One. God is the Wholly Other, but he is powerful enough
to be able to show himself. And he has so fashioned his
creature that it is capable of 'seeing' him and loving him."[23]

---

[22] Ratzinger, *Spirit of the Liturgy*, p. 123.
[23] Ibid., pp. 123–24.

Let us be frank: the new churches being built are sometimes functional but incapable of transmitting the beauty of God, so they are rarely beautiful. There is nothing to do but to ask "for the gift of a new kind of seeing. And so it would be worth our while to regain a faith that sees. Wherever that exists, art finds its proper expression." [24]

Art merits the title "sacred" if it permits man to be touched by the presence of God, that is, God's divine reality. Does this happen by itself? It does not seem to. The liturgy that is bereft of the sacred, of the sense of the divine presence in our midst, has brought about the loss of a taste for the beautiful on the part of many priests and faithful. Has not the use of churches for concerts, comedies, and even interreligious celebrations become—in a troubling way—a widespread practice since the Council? This was something we had known to occur only under atheist regimes. What about the dedication of a church, that act whereby the building is removed from the sphere of the profane and offered totally to God? For many, the church is no longer the place where God dwells and where we his people go to adore him; it is, rather, a multipurpose facility. Above the entrance to a church in my city is written: *Iesu redemptori sacrum.* Does this still mean something today?

It all began after the Council. The linear form that was typical of Catholic church buildings, with the longitudinal nave and the presbytery more or less elevated, was interpreted as a distancing of the people. The semicircle or "theater in the round" form was then championed, which gives the impression of the indispensability of the people for the celebration and permits open conversation. It is a shame

---

[24] Ibid., p. 135.

that this happened while many people silently distanced themselves from the Church. Our looking at each other in the liturgy has taken our gaze away from God. Church naves that lift our eyes up—"nave" means space moving toward the destination, looking ahead and up—help us to advance, to proceed toward the goal that is the Lord; naves favored the processions of the liturgy. In Christian antiquity, the circular form was reserved solely for the preservation of some sacred object around which pilgrimages were made: the prototype is the Holy Sepulcher in Jerusalem, but the basilica with a nave served for liturgical celebrations.

It is true that the Church is also the house of the people of God, but it is first of all the house *of God*, of his presence and, with him, of all his family, the saints. He lives in communion. The presence of Mary, the saints, and the dead helps us to understand that God's presence is not solitary. People entering church in the East and the West greet God's family members before they approach the Lord, who is head of the household.

The misunderstanding of the Church as entirely ministerial led to the abolition of the distinction between the nave and the presbytery (Robert Hugh Benson's foresight is striking[25] as are Guareschi's observations in letters to Don Camillo written after the Council[26]). That was one way to signal the abolition of the sacred and also to nullify the distinction between clergy and faithful. And yet, the *General Instruction of the Roman Missal* prescribes that the presbytery should be suitably distinguished from the nave of the church by means of elevation or through

[25] Robert Hugh Benson, *By What Authority?* (London: Isbister and Company, 1904).

[26] Alberto and Carlotta Guareschi, *Le lampade e la luce* (Milan: Rizzoli, 1996).

special ornamentation,[27] which might be done with a railing and gates, for example. At Mount Athos, Catholics are normally permitted only in the first part of the church, the narthex, because the narthex is reserved for catechumens and penitents. But these latter are not allowed in the nave (*naos*), which culminates before the iconostasis that delimits the sanctuary. The *naos* is for those who are admitted to eucharistic Communion. Some Catholic churches have begun to restrict tourists and visitors to certain parts of the church. Perhaps the same might be done with regard to non-Catholics and non-Christians. If we want to promote ecumenism, let us restore the distinctions.

In a paper given in 1960, Hans Urs von Balthasar describes the Church living in an incomprehensible place between earth and heaven, between death and eternal life, between the old world that is passing and the new world that is without end. The apse, with the episcopal cathedra and the seats for the clergy—the priest with the ministers—recalls the hierarchical nature of the Church and is distinct from the nave, where the faithful take their place; the centrality of the altar beneath the triumphal arch, between the columns of the canopy (the ciborium), is the doctrine of the primacy of the worship of the eucharistic sacrifice; the ambo placed at edge of the presbytery with the nave indicates the proclamation of the Gospel to the ends of the earth; the orientation of the building toward the rising of the light—like the octagon of the baptistery—indicates that those who are oriented to eternal life are reborn.

---

[27] Cf. *General Instruction of the Roman Missal*, no. 295.

Such symbolism helps the very human movement from the sensory to the spiritual, from the terrestrial to the eternal, from the creature to the Creator. Should we abandon the image of the Church-body, who, with Christ as head, engages in spiritual worship, offering our bodies in spiritual sacrifice? Should we reduce the presbytery to a foyer into which everyone enters?

VII

A NEW LITURGICAL MOVEMENT

Liturgical Formation

Benedict XVI's thought about the renewal of the liturgy desired by the Council, shared by the majority of bishops, is that it contains riches that have not yet been fully explored.[1] So, the liturgical reform is still far from perfect and complete: there is need for corrections and integrations; however, we must proceed in a different way from that followed in the initial postconciliar period, not imposing obligations except for those that are necessary, illustrating possibilities and promoting debate.

To recover the liturgical movement, we must familiarize ourselves with the theological fundamentals of the liturgy described in a systematic way by the *Catechism of the Catholic Church*[2] on the basis of the constitution *Sacrosanctum concilium*. This will help us identify textual and liturgical aspects that need to be restored.

Not a few priests understand the liturgy as something to be constructed according to their own ideas. There are many

---

[1] Cf. Benedict XVI, Post-synodal Apostolic Exhortation *Sacramentum caritatis* (February 22, 2007), no. 3.
[2] CCC 1077–1112.

documents of the Congregation for Divine Worship, but they go unapplied because there is a crisis of obedience. And yet the bishops are aware of the duty, especially on pastoral visits, to correct abuses and recall canonical sanctions. It would be possible, as the Church has always done in cases of emergency, to appoint an "apostolic visitor" for the liturgy. This would be for the current generation of clergy.

For the new generations: the rectors of seminaries and the heads of theology faculties need to be aware of the "deformations" and of the "right way to celebrate"—the famous *ars celebrandi*—so that they take this into account in the formation of seminarians and priests. In this regard, we must return to teaching how to celebrate the sacraments, and the divine Eucharist in particular. The fear of reducing the liturgy to ceremony has led to the elimination of training in liturgical celebration; although only a few seminaries have retained this, it constitutes, on the contrary, in the years of formation, above all when ordination is in view, a solid school and an optimal antidote to the conception of a liturgy created "from below".

Furthermore, we need to promote meetings of priests and seminarians with ecclesial movements that are more positive about and attentive to the discipline of the Church.

We need to explain that the liturgy is *sacred* and *divine*, that it descends from heaven like the heavenly Jerusalem; the priest celebrates it in the person of Christ the head, living in the Church, inasmuch as he is the intermediary minister. The term "liturgy" indicates the "action of the holy people", in the sense that they participate in the sacred action, uniting their offering to the sacrifice of Jesus Christ. Alongside the liturgy, we need to reintroduce the term "cult", or "worship", in a suitable way. This term indicates man's "cultivated" relation of reverence and adoration with God.

On this point in particular, a study of the ecclesiological and liturgical magisterium of Pius XII could help (the encyclicals *Mystici Corporis* and *Mediator Dei*) and the liturgical tradition of the East: the constitution *Missale Romanum* explicitly suggests it as a repository of a great wealth of piety and doctrine. One thinks, to recall only the Byzantine liturgy, of the long and repetitive penitential prayers; of the solemn rites of vesting of the celebrant and the deacon; of the preparation of the offerings, which is already a complete rite in itself; of the constant presence, in the prayers—even in the special particle of the prosphora that commemorates her during the liturgy of preparation—of the Blessed Virgin, of the saints and the angelic hierarchies (which in the procession of the Gospel book are evoked as invisibly concelebrating and with whom the choir identifies itself in the singing of the Cherubic hymn); of the iconostasis that clearly distinguishes the sanctuary from the temple, the clergy from the people; of the consecration that is often hidden by the curtain, an obvious symbol of the Unknowable to which the whole liturgy alludes; of the position of the celebrant *versus Deum* each time he prays; of the Communion that is administered always and only by the celebrant; of the continuous and profound gestures of adoration that are made in the presence of the Sacred Species; of the essentially contemplative attitude of the people. The fact that such a liturgy, even in the less solemn forms, lasts for quite some time and is defined as "tremendous and unspeakable", "tremendous, celestial, life-giving mysteries", and so on, is enough to show the understanding that the East has of it, which is something on which those of the Latin Rite might meditate.

There might be occasions for presenting the Roman liturgy in a comparative way with the Eastern liturgies, highlighting the ecumenical consequences, since the Patriarch of Moscow has expressed approval of the initiative of Benedict XVI in restoring the tradition with the *motu proprio*. In this way, the fear about the coexistence of diverse ritual forms would be attenuated. One already finds various examples in the Roman Missal of Paul VI, such as the rite for the adoration of the cross on Good Friday, which can be done in two forms. So, the solution to the need to safeguard the old rite, proposing rather than imposing it, has already been found. Catholic unity is expressed precisely through the complementarity of diverse ritual forms.

It has been proposed that priests do the offertory and the anaphora turned to the cross, exhorting the faithful to assume the same attitude of adoration; this can be done especially in the seasons of Advent and Lent in order to underscore the eschatological dimension of the liturgy. In those places where the altar is turned *toward the people* and there is little space behind it, there can be an exception; or the cross can be suspended above the altar or placed in the center, in front of it or on it, in a way that allows both the priest and the faithful to look at it. It should be explained that the cross is not a mere decoration that blocks one's line of sight but the image that is most essential for prayer, guiding physical and interior vision.

From such premises emerge the fundamental issues or priorities for intervention set down by Benedict XVI's postsynodal exhortation *Sacramentum caritatis*:

- The "newness" of the form of the Eucharist,[3] which in itself is the Church's greatest act of adoration;[4]

[3] *Sacramentum caritatis*, nos. 10–11.
[4] Ibid., no. 66; cf. CCC 1078.

- the centrality of the tabernacle:[5] its history evidences the awareness reached by the Church that the mystery is always present because it comes *before* everything else: I am the one who must make myself present to him with adoration; it is his permanent presence that continually reawakens my faith, not my own capacities. Christ has come into the world to be with us all days. We cannot retreat from this awareness. Christ remains present in his Church by the power of the Holy Spirit starting with the Eucharist;[6] he is present in the word, "when the holy scriptures are read in the Church".[7] Christ is not present in the book of the Scriptures or in the book of the Gospels: it is venerated—not adored—because it is a sign that points to him but is not he.

The widespread custom of keeping the lectionary open on the ambo has a similar—but not the same—meaning as the permanent placement of the tabernacle on the altar (in some places the book of Gospels is in fact placed on a stand above the tabernacle).

At the beginning of the postconciliar reform, the tabernacle was not thought to be an obstacle to Mass celebrated *facing the people*. The liturgical instructions, indeed, say that "Mass may be celebrated facing the people even though there is a tabernacle on the altar, provided this is small but adequate."[8]

---

[5] *Sacramentum caritatis*, no. 69.

[6] Ibid., no. 12.

[7] Ibid., no. 45.

[8] *Consilium*, Instruction on Implementing Liturgical Norms *Inter oecumenici* (September 26, 1964), no. 95, and Sacred Congregation of Rites, Instruction on Eucharistic Worship *Eucharisticum Mysterium* (May 25, 1967), no. 54.

But the idea began to catch on that Jesus' presence
in the tabernacle on the altar on which Mass was
celebrated was not appropriate, since he became
present in this way in the Consecration; thus, insofar as it is possible, it was suggested that it be removed
"as a sign".[9] Apparently, this was not a wise decision. It happened that the majority of the faithful
are no longer able to distinguish the "different" or
"principal" "modes of Christ's presence"[10] and think
of them as more or less the same thing: relativism
entered in here before it did elsewhere. For this reason, it became necessary to amend the instruction
on the Missal,[11] taking up the above once again.

The Christian liturgy is beautiful by its nature[12] and remains
such if all of its parts (rite, vestments ... art, song) are in
harmony,[13] thus:

- the homily must relate word and sacrament, transmitting the doctrine of the Church;[14] the word of
  God is contained in Scripture but includes the tradition, which is also a source of revelation. The homily should transmit the teaching of the Church, of
  the Pope and the bishops united with him, and it
  must bring the listeners to reflect on the principal
  themes of the Creed, of the sacraments, of the moral
  life, and of prayer (see the primary divisions of the

[9] *Eucharisticum Mysterium*, no. 55.
[10] Cf. ibid., nos. 9 and 55.
[11] *General Instruction of the Roman Missal*, no. 314.
[12] *Sacramentum caritatis*, no. 35.
[13] Ibid., nos. 40–52.
[14] Ibid., no. 46, n. 143.

Catechism). The homily and the Liturgy of the Word together should not last longer than the eucharistic liturgy.

- the different place of the sign of peace[15] in the Roman Rite and in the Eastern Rites must be considered; it is not superfluous to recall that the kiss of peace is a sacred action because it signifies the unity between us and especially with the Word, communion, and charity.[16] Because peace is first of all asked for with a prayer—before communion in the Roman Rite—the exchange of the gesture among those present is not obligatory but must be determined according to the situation.[17] The Roman Rite maintains the ancient meaning that this part of the liturgy had for the first Christians: peace as synonymous with eucharistic communion, because through the Lord barriers are overcome and men are gathered into a new unity.

- the recourse to concelebration, especially when many priests are present, should be reevaluated;[18] the Council itself saw it as limited, and it has never been made an obligation;[19] it promotes the perception of the unity of the priesthood in the Church around the bishop, but, if it is practiced too frequently, it hinders the understanding of the mediating function of the individual priest, who, as we said earlier, is not merely

---

[15] Ibid., no. 49, n. 150.
[16] Cf. Congregation for Divine Worship and the Discipline of the Sacraments (see p. 56, FN 13), Instruction *Redemptionis sacramentum* (March 25, 2004), no. 71.
[17] *General Instruction of the Roman Missal*, no. 56b.
[18] *Sacramentum caritatis*, no. 61.
[19] Second Vatican Council, Constitution on the Sacred Liturgy *Sacrosanctum concilium* (December 4, 1963), no. 57; *Code of Canon Law*, can. 902.

the president of the assembly; furthermore, it deprives
the faithful of being able to participate in the Mass in
more places and times since the priests do not celebrate separate Masses. Thus, the slogan "more Mass
and fewer Masses" is very ambiguous and should be
dropped;

- future priests should receive the necessary formation
to be able to understand and celebrate the Mass in
Latin.[20]

At the same time, every Christian must be helped to correspond to the nature of the liturgy.

Faith is the indispensable condition for participation in the
liturgy, which means:[21]

a. having an awareness of the mystery to the point of making an offering of oneself;[22] this is the true realization of
Christ's sacrifice in us;[23]

b. celebrating in an interiorly active way: this is the ultimate point of mystagogical catechesis;[24] which means, above
all, reverence[25] and adoration.[26] All of this is a fundamental condition for receiving communion.[27]

[20] *Sacramentum caritatis*, no. 62.
[21] Ibid., no. 6.
[22] Ibid., no. 52.
[23] Ibid., nos. 70–71.
[24] Ibid., no. 64.
[25] Ibid., no. 65.
[26] Ibid., no. 66.
[27] Cf. ibid., no. 29.

Ecclesial membership is the other prior condition for participation:[28]

a. such membership flows from the connection between the Eucharist and the Catholic Church,[29] which constitute the "whole Christ":[30] this means that the marks of the Church—one, holy, catholic, apostolic—must shine forth in the liturgy; more than inculturation, we must speak of the intercultural nature of the liturgy;[31]

b. that which we hand on, the Apostle says, is a doctrine that is not our own (concept of tradition);[32]

c. membership is expressed publicly before the people of God with the priest's obedience to the norms of the liturgy and with the bishop seeing that they are respected;[33] the liturgical norms and institutions stem from the Lord's will—one thinks of the minute instructions that he gave to the disciples for preparing the Last Supper. He is their original author, and so they must be given joyful obedience. Disobedience to the liturgical norms is immoral and derives from a false concept of freedom[34] because it follows the dominant culture, which seeks to be without rules or fixed points, something that is also at the root of the deterioration of public and private morality. The *lex orandi* is the law, that is, the discipline of the liturgy. If this is not understood, then rubricism and legalism,

---

[28] Ibid., no. 76.
[29] Ibid., nos. 14–15.
[30] Ibid., no. 36.
[31] Ibid., no. 78.
[32] Cf. ibid., no. 37.
[33] Ibid., nos. 38–39.
[34] *Redemptionis sacramentum*, no. 7.

which receive so much scorn, will be replaced by anarchy and lawlessness, which are worse. Obedience to the sacred liturgy is the measure of our humility.

d. If the priest acts *in the person of Christ*, in the liturgy he must be and appear humble like him.[35]

The "conditions" for receiving Communion must be recalled;[36] reception in the hand must be rethought;[37] spiritual communion and, before this, ecclesial communion, must be rediscovered.[38] Joseph Ratzinger recalls that "Eucharist presupposes baptism; it presupposes continual recourse to the sacrament of penance. The Holy Father has emphasized this most strongly in his encyclical '*Redemptor Hominis*'. The first element of the Good News, he stresses, was 'Repent!' 'The Christ who invites us to the eucharistic meal is always the same Christ who exhorts us to penance, continually saying "Repent!" ' (IV, 20). Where penance disappears, the Eucharist is no longer discerned and, as the Lord's Eucharist, is destroyed." [39]

It would be desirable in the whole Church to restore on Wednesday of Holy Week the rite of the reconciliation of penitents with individual confession in order to promote awareness of and put into practice what we have said.

The objective of active participation in the liturgy is the efficaciousness of Christ's sacrifice in us;[40] the "worship

---

[35] *Sacramentum caritatis*, no. 23; cf. *Missale Romanum, editio typica* I, no. 23; III, no. 60.

[36] *Sacramentum caritatis*, nos. 29, 50.

[37] Ibid., nos. 50–55.

[38] Ibid., no. 56.

[39] Cf. J. Ratzinger, *The Feast of Faith: Approaches to a Theology of the Liturgy*, trans. G. Harrison (San Francisco: Ignatius Press, 1986), p. 152.

[40] *Sacramentum caritatis*, nos. 70–71.

pleasing to God" that, through testimony[41] and martyr-dom,[42] brings God to man in Christ the one Savior.[43]

The Eucharist brings about the moral transformation of man,[44] that is, sanctification and "divinization"; for this reason, "eucharistic consistency" is required.

The blood of Christ is the price of man's dignity; from this flow the social implications of the Eucharist.[45]

With these theological and liturgical premises, the principal "deformations" can be confronted:

a. the transformation of the liturgy from prayer or dialogue with God into the *exhibition* of actors and the *multiplication* of words: this is encouraged by the fact that the priest, facing the people, is easily led to turn his gaze toward them instead of raising it up or toward the cross, as prayerful dialogue with God would demand; thus the hymns, the psalms, the penitential act, the collects, the prayers of the faithful, and above all the anaphora, which means *sacrificial prayer*, are perceived as a recitation, and not a very serious one, since it is often interrupted to exhort and instruct the faithful;

b. the condemnation of the concept of sacrifice, replaced by that of meal, which has made the Catholic Eucharist similar to the celebration of the Protestant supper;

c. the disorientation created by the recitation of the anaphora *versus populum*, which has helped to confirm that the Mass is a fraternal meal;

[41] Ibid., no. 79.
[42] Ibid., no. 85.
[43] Ibid., no. 86.
[44] Ibid., nos. 82–83.
[45] Ibid., nos. 89–91.

d. the complete replacement of Latin with the vernacular;

e. the "artistic" revolution that has led in particular to changing the form of the altar into a table and to decentralizing the tabernacle, replacing it with the priest's chair—the priest becoming ever more the focus—to say nothing of the abolition of the sacred enclosure of the sanctuary and the removal of the baptismal font to the presbytery.

Translations and the Case of the Pro Multis

The Church's tradition is also transmitted through the translation of liturgical texts into the vernacular. The word "translate" (*tradurre*) is linked to the Latin term *tradere* (to hand on) but also at the risk of betraying (*tradire*). We all know about the accusations of superficiality—and, worse still, of ideological deviations and invasions—that have been made in regard to different translations of the Roman Missal in the postconciliar period, especially English translations. There are documents of the Congregation for Divine Worship that provide guidance, but they are not always followed. Who is aware of the October 17, 2006, letter sent to the bishops by the cardinal prefect of the congregation, Francis Arinze, about changing the expression "for many" (*pro multis*) to "for all" in the formula of the consecration of the bread and wine in the Holy Mass?

On the issue of the proper translation of *pro multis*, Joseph Ratzinger has made three important observations:[46]

---

[46] Cf. *God Is Near Us: The Eucharist, the Heart of Life*, trans. H. Taylor (San Francisco: Ignatius Press, 2003), pp. 35–41.

1. Jesus died to save all, and this is not something Christians can deny.

2. God lovingly permits man in his freedom to refuse salvation, and some do this.

3. "The fact that in Hebrew the expression 'many' would mean the same thing as 'all' is not relevant to the question under consideration inasmuch as it is a question of translating, not a Hebrew text here, but a Latin text (from the Roman Liturgy), which is directly related to a Greek text (the New Testament). The institution narratives in the New Testament are by no means simply a translation (still less, a mistaken translation) of Isaiah; rather, they constitute an independent source." [47]

In conclusion, the letter of Cardinal Arinze invites the bishops' conferences to catechize the faithful to prepare them for the introduction of the exact translation of the formula *pro multis* (for example, "for many", "per molti", and so on) in the various vernaculars in the next edition of the Roman Missal that the bishops and the Holy See approve for use in those countries. The instruction *Liturgiam authenticam* asked that translations be consistent with the "meaning" and "theological content" of the typical editions." [48]

The Council, Latin, and Gregorian Chant

Blessed John XXIII asserted that if the Catholic truths were simply entrusted to modern languages, which are still

[47] Ibid., pp. 37–38, n. 10.
[48] Congregation for Divine Worship and the Discipline of the Sacraments, Instruction *Liturgiam authenticam*, no. 107.

subject to change as they continue to be in use, the sense of these truths would not be manifested with sufficient clarity and precision. Without Latin, he observed, the Church would lack a common and stable language with which to compare the others.[49] Latin, thus, safeguards doctrine insofar as it is no longer subject to changes. We know that "[i]n the liturgy every word and every gesture expresses an idea which is always a theological idea." [50]

For 1,600 years Latin has been the official language of the Roman Catholic Church, just as Greek has been for the Church of Constantinople, Church Slavonic for Russian Orthodoxy, and medieval German for Lutherans. Latin is therefore also the language of the Roman liturgy, as it is for other Western liturgies: it is a sign of ecclesial unity that transcends time and space, because it links the Christian generations of the first centuries to those of today and because it allows all Catholics to join in one voice; it is the universal Church that prays through the mouths of her children without distinction of race or culture.

We cannot forget, on the other hand, that, as in the Eastern liturgies, the participation of the faithful must be more direct and conscious. On the basis of the experiences of the years preceding the Council, the constitution on the liturgy pronounced wisely on the matter: first of all, it called for the preservation of Latin in the Latin liturgies without prejudice to particular law,[51] especially the canon; that the faithful know how to recite and sing their parts in Latin[52]

---

[49] John XXIII, Apostolic Constitution *Veterum sapientia* (February 22, 1962).

[50] N. Giampietro, *The Development of the Liturgical Reform as Seen by Cardinal Ferdinando Antonelli from 1948–1970* (Fort Collins, Colo.: Roman Catholic Books, 2009), pp. 191, 196.

[51] *Sacrosanctum concilium*, no. 36.

[52] Ibid., no. 54.

as in the vernacular; that the clergy know how to recite the office in Latin according to the tradition;[53] for other parts, such as the readings and the prayers of the faithful, the use of the vernacular was foreseen.

What happened? In regard to what was translated into the vernacular, many liturgical texts could not be rendered with the same effectiveness, to say nothing of Gregorian chant and the polyphony connected with it. Furthermore, the thesis (positive in itself) about inculturating the liturgy in a given place cannot supplant the thesis that precedes and follows it: the liturgy must express the unity and catholicity of the Church. The tension between universality and the multiplicity of cultures, precisely the so-called multicultural society, cannot be resolved by questioning the universal structure of human experience. Ratzinger held that translating the liturgy into the vernacular was a good thing, because we must understand it; we must take part in it even with our thought; but the more marked presence of some elements in Latin would help to provide the universal dimension, to make it so that in every part of the world one can say: "I am in the same Church" ... to have a greater experience of universality, not to exclude the possibility of communication between speakers of different languages, which is a very precious thing in regions with mixed populations.[54] With Latin, priests can say Mass in any part of the world and be understood.

Surreptitiously, however, the thesis of the centuries-old incommunicability of the liturgy has been advanced along

---

[53] Ibid., no. 101. This was confirmed by the Second Vatican Council, Decree on Priestly Training *Optatam totius* (October 28, 1965), no. 13; documents of application such as *Sapientia christiana*, IV, no. 24, 3; and the *Code of Canon Law*, cann. 249, 928.

[54] J. Ratzinger, *God and the World: A Conversation with Peter Seewald*, trans. H. Taylor (San Francisco: Ignatius Press, 2002), p. 417.

with the thesis that at the time of Trent almost no priest understood Latin. What has been forgotten is the work of formation of the clergy and the catechesis of the faithful launched by that council, which in four centuries changed the situation. This thesis is silent about the fact that our fathers lived the eucharistic and liturgical mystery more deeply than we do today, and it ultimately means denying the action of the Holy Spirit. Is understanding the mystery not discerning the presence of Christ on the altar and falling on our knees, annihilated, like Peter and exclaiming, "Depart from me, a sinner"? Despite having the liturgy in the vernacular, the number of faithful in churches is quite diminished: perhaps, some say, because they did not like what they understood. Divo Barsotti asks: "Do we think we will understand something more about the essence and mystery of the Eucharist if we only and always speak in the vernacular? The problem is not merely understanding something intellectually but having a real encounter with Christ." [55]

In many parts of the world there is a return to Latin: from Oxford to Cambridge, to Seattle ... Why think of it as backwardness? Europeans must learn English to communicate with the world. Might it not be useful for a Catholic to learn Latin, his mother tongue, to communicate in the liturgy with his brothers in the faith and to know how to decipher our Church's musical and artistic patrimony without acting illiterate? All religions use a sacred language: ancient Arabic for the Muslims, Sanskrit for the Hindus. So, we should not be afraid of Latin: young people understand it and crowd into the Masses in Latin. In

[55] D. Barsotti, *I cristiani vogliono essere cristiani* (Cinisello Balsamo: San Paolo, 2006), pp. 269–71.

the Holy See's *recognitio*, then, of the national Missals, it could be demanded that the text of the ordinary be published in bilingual editions: Latin and the vernacular together in the same volume as in the 1962 Roman Missal.

As we said, Latin and Gregorian chant were condemned together. The latter was abandoned in the liturgy because "no one could understand it"—so it is odd that it is becoming more and more popular in concerts and in pop music. The strange idea was circulated that dispensing with solemnity and beauty when in God's presence conformed the liturgy more to God. Recalling the confrontation of the early Church with the Greek world and the Council of Laodicea's prohibition in canon 59 of private and non-canonical compositions,[56] Ratzinger points out that the undiscerning introduction of new poetry and music into the liturgy runs the risk of watering down the Christian event into a kind of general mysticism, as happened in the first centuries. Several times we have explained that Christian worship is rational, logical, because it is inspired by the *Logos*, or Word made flesh. Only the spirit that recognizes Jesus as the Lord who has come in the flesh— Paul and John say—is spirit and truth; otherwise it is the spirit of error. Not a few musicians and composers ask whether the songs and melodies that are entering our churches follow this criterion.[57]

Song must be sacred: joyous and jubilant, without unseemliness, poetic and noble, without artifice, sweet and mellifluous, without affectation or sentimentalism. It has been observed that we have come to the point of setting the text of the Our Father, a prayer taught by Jesus

---

[56] J. Ratzinger, *The Spirit of the Liturgy*, trans. J. Saward (San Francisco: Ignatius Press, 2000), p. 144.

[57] Ibid., pp. 150–51.

himself, to the melody of Simon and Garfunkel's "The Sound of Silence", or to brush up John Lennon's "Imagine", whose lyrics envision a world without heaven or religion, for a eucharistic congress. The order of the day seems to be nice tunes, the idea of peace without foundation or substance, and a dreamy atmosphere. It is as if to oppose modern rationalism, cynicism, materialism, and unbelief, it is necessary to take refuge in a romantic rhetoric of good feelings, in a languid debilitation of the senses and the mind, which in reality has nothing to do with the evangelical virtues. Are we not in the presence of an undifferentiated romantic and subjective decline? We are nearing gnosticism in liturgical music. With the people no longer singing and the Protestantized music, the idea of what the Eucharist is—a physical and spiritual encounter with Christ—has been lost. The Mass has been reduced to listening to the word and remembering a past event.

Naturally, we must not believe that Christian sacred music no longer exists, but we must not suppose—following a New Age tendency—that all music is sacred, religious, in a strict sense, or in fact Christian. It is possible that the distance from the faith and dissonance of certain contemporary music is synonymous with nihilism, as Olivier Messiaen believed, but the sacred music in the liturgy draws from the uniqueness of Christian worship, which, unlike other religious cults, has a clear responsorial position: God speaks and man listens and answers; this is the course followed by Christian sacred song: to the point of being in *reasonable* consonance with him who is the *Logos*. Christian music must reveal the truth; it must be the elevated and complete expression of the prayer of the Church, not individual sentiment. Certainly there is the first stage, the subjectivity of the voice that comes from the soul and sings, but it must flow into, and in a certain sense recreate itself, in the objectivity of the Word. The liturgical musician must have a knowledge of music and the Christian faith in order to reach the towering summit of being in tune with the mystery celebrated. This is the canon or rule for music that is permitted entry into the divine Christian liturgy. If, among the various types of Gregorian chant that were in circulation during the medieval period, only one achieved citizenship, it means that it passed the test we have mentioned and remained with us. Could it be otherwise today? Often with my old friend Anselmo Susca, a Benedictine monk and distinguished scholar in Gregorian chant, I have discussed whether there is anything "active" in listening, intuiting, in being moved. Is it possible that modern sacred music has become suitable for use? The celebration must maintain a phonic, homogeneous equilibrium. Thus in the prayers and songs a subdued voice is better; it is consonant with the attitude of humility and discretion that we must have before God. Thus, brash tones must be carefully avoided and more subdued tones cultivated, proper to the prayer said "in secret" (cf. Mt 6:5). In that sense, the monastic liturgy should be considered the one to which we turn for inspiration. Thus, beginning with the priest who leads the people, Gregorian chant for the ordinary of the Mass—which is already often done in the vernacular—should be recovered and perhaps some parts of the proper, especially for solemnities.

Silence in the liturgy, which is essential for listening to God, who speaks to our heart, is prior to music and what makes it possible. The soul is not for noise and debate but for recollection; the fact that noise bothers us is a sign of this. Above all, it is necessary to restore to the church its dignity as a sacred temple where no one speaks in a loud voice, starting with the priests and ministers, but everyone must turn to God in humble silence and a hushed voice. It is necessary to have the courage to keep all that is repulsive to the faith or offends the true religious sense far from the sanctuary.

The Second Vatican Council states that "[t]he musical tradition of the universal Church is a treasure of inestimable value, greater even than that of any other art. The main reason for this pre-eminence is that, as sacred song united to the words, it forms a necessary or integral part of the solemn liturgy",[58] and concludes: "The Church acknowledges Gregorian chant as specially suited to the Roman liturgy: therefore, other things being equal, it should be given pride of place in liturgical services." [59] John Paul II confirmed the "general law" formulated by Pius X: "The more closely a composition for church approaches in its movement, inspiration and savor the Gregorian melodic form, the more sacred and liturgical it becomes; and the more out of harmony it is with that supreme model, the less worthy it is of the temple." [60]

Gregorian chant, which has been unjustly abandoned for too many years, belongs to this liturgical patrimony *in primis*. According to Joseph Ratzinger, "the retreat into utility has not made the liturgy more open; it has only impoverished it." [61] Liturgical music must have a subdued tone; its purpose is not to seek applause but edification. Saint Jerome rebuked vanity and the seeking of effect in artists' exhibitions.

Benedict XVI expresses a wish that is both a plea and an authoritative instruction: "I desire, in accordance with the

[58] *Sacrosanctum concilium*, no. 112.

[59] Ibid., no. 116.

[60] John Paul II, "Chirograph for the Centenary of the Motu Proprio *Tra le Sollecitudini* on Sacred Music" (November 22, 2003), no. 12.

[61] Ratzinger, *Feast of Faith*, p. 101.

request advanced by the Synod Fathers, that Gregorian chant be suitably esteemed and employed as the chant proper to the Roman liturgy." [62] Thus, "I ask that future priests, from their time in the seminary, receive the preparation needed to understand and to celebrate Mass in Latin, and also to use Latin texts and execute Gregorian chant." [63] And the faithful, too, should be taught "to sing parts of the liturgy in Gregorian chant". [64]

With the Patience of Love

A new liturgical movement is being born that looks to the liturgies of Benedict XVI; instructions prepared by experts are not enough. There must be exemplary liturgies that make an encounter with God possible. But those who are purposefully superficial are not embracing this movement. It is a new beginning that has been born from the depths of the liturgy, just as was the liturgical movement of the last century, which culminated with the Council. The liturgy is here understood as an encounter with the living God, not a show to make religion interesting, not a museum of grandiose ritual gestures. The people of God celebrates the new rite with respect and solemnity but is disoriented by the contradictions of the two extremes. The liturgy will return to being an ecclesial action, not through the work of specialists and liturgical teams, but through priests and laypeople who, because of their knowledge of the sources, consider the Western liturgy as the

[62] *Sacramentum caritatis*, no. 42.
[63] Ibid., no. 62.
[64] Ibid.

fruit of historical development and the Eastern liturgy a reflection of the eternal. The ancient Fathers and the medieval masters were opposed to the mystification of the liturgy, and, knowing the history, they have shown us the multiple forms of its path. The Holy Father has gathered up the legacy of the preconciliar liturgical movement and made it bear fruit; he has pursued the goal of allowing the old and the new forms of the Roman Rite to coexist alongside each other as was already the case with the Ambrosian and Eastern Rites.

Let us put our trust in him: he patiently carries the wisdom of the Catholic imagination in the life of the modern Church. He understands well that innovation is not hostile to tradition but is part of it, like the lifeblood of the Holy Spirit. He is neither a conservative nor an innovator, but a missionary "humble worker in the vineyard of the Lord". In the book *Jesus of Nazareth*, he underscores the "understanding" that in the Gospel of Luke—unlike the other Gospels—Jesus shows for the Israelites:

> I find particularly significant the way he concludes the story of the new wine and the old or new wineskins. In Mark we find, "And no one puts new wine into old wineskins; if he does, the wine will burst the skins, and the wine is lost, and so are the skins; but new wine is for fresh skins" (Mk 2:22). The text reads similarly in Matthew 9:17. Luke transmits to us the same saying, but at the end he adds: "And no one after drinking old wine desires new; for he says, 'The old is good'" (Lk 5:39). There do seem to be good grounds for interpreting this as a word of understanding for those who wished to remain with the "old wine".[65]

[65] J. Ratzinger, *Jesus of Nazareth: From the Baptism in the Jordan to the Transfiguration*, trans. A. Walker (New York et al.: Doubleday, 2008), p. 181.

Is this parable not applicable to the debate over the *usus antiquior* and the *usus novus* of the Mass that followed the *motu proprio?*

The Christian liturgy, and the Christian event itself, are not made by us. The term "actualization" gave rise to the idea that we have the capacity to replicate it, to create the right conditions for it to take place, that we almost make what we claim to believe. In reality, it is Jesus Christ who makes the sacred liturgy with the Holy Spirit. It is our job to follow, to make space for his work. The method available to everyone is to look upon what is happening—one used to say "assist", that is, *ad-stare*, stand in the presence of; it means to conform to Something that comes before, to follow that which he is doing in our midst. This should make it clear that worship is not created by us. The liturgy is sacred and divine because it is a Thing that comes from the other world.

We want to help with the understanding and worthy celebration of the liturgy as a possibility for an encounter with the reality of God and the cause of man's morality, to diagnose the degradations that are a symptom of spiritual emptiness, indicating the path to the restoration of the spirit in the sign of the unity of apostolic and catholic faith, to promote a serious debate and an educational journey following the thought and the example of the Pope, who is relaunching the liturgical movement. We need to grasp the spirit of the liturgy as adoration of God the Father through Jesus Christ in the Holy Spirit and as pedagogy for entering into the mystery and being transformed morally and in terms of sanctity. It is also an invitation to non-believers who are nevertheless desirous of the true, because no one is immune to the doubt that perhaps there is Someone else who exists to whom we should dedicate our time! Upon this "perhaps", which the liturgy does not totally unveil—this is why one asks that the sense of mystery and the sacred be maintained—communication between believers and non-believers (or those who believe differently) will be built.

I cordially thank Vittorio Messori, with whom I shared many of these reflections and who, with his wife, Rosanna, encouraged me in this work. He also has my admiration for having foreseen with Joseph Ratzinger in *The Ratzinger Report* this time "in which patience, that daily form of love, is called for. A love in which faith and hope are simultaneously present." [66]

So, we must hope for the coming of what the Holy Father spoke of in the conclusion of his homily for the Feast of Saints Peter and Paul in 2008: "When the world in all its parts has become a liturgy of God, when, in its reality, it has become adoration, then it will have reached its goal and will be safe and sound. This is the ultimate goal of Saint Paul's apostolic mission and of our own mission. The Lord calls us to this ministry. Let us pray at this time that he may help us carry it out properly, to become true liturgists of Jesus Christ."

---

[66] J. Ratzinger and V. Messori, *The Ratzinger Report: An Exclusive Interview on the State of the Church*, trans. S. Attanasio and G. Harrison (San Francisco: Ignatius Press, 1985). p. 14.

INDEX

altar: altar-placement and the
Cross, 42, 122–24, 134; and
Benedict XVI's new liturgical
movement, 135–36, 142; conciliar reform and adaptations
to, 69–70, 122–24, 134, 135–
36, 142; and position of the
priest's chair, 123–24, 142; and
the tabernacle, 69–70, 135–36,
142
Ambrose, Saint, 37
"amen", 32
"anthropological turn", 31, 73–74
antiquarianism, 61–62, 73
Antonelli, Ferdinando, 64–66, 73
Arinze, Francis, 142–43
art and the sacred: images in the
liturgy, 125–26; and mystery,
124–30; role of the senses in
the liturgy, 126–27; and the
sacrality of the Church
building, 124–30; Schönborn
on, 125
Augustine, Saint, 29, 35

baptismal rite, 42, 73, 84, 140
Barsotti, Divo, 146
Basil the Great, Saint, 88, 122
Basilica of Hagia Sophia
(Constantinople), 112
Benedict XV, Pope, 83
Benedict XVI, Pope: on the con-
ditions for receiving commu-

nion, 138–40; on Gregorian
chant and liturgical music,
150–51; homily for the
Chrism Mass in Saint Peter's
Basilica (2008), 114–16; homily
for the Feast of Saints Peter
and Paul (2008), 154; homily
on the priestly service and the
Eucharistic celebration, 114–
16; on influence of modernity
and rationalism on Christianity,
112–13; and Latin language/
vernacular, 138, 142, 143–47;
Letter to the Bishops on occasion of publication of the *motu
proprio*, 78–85, 102; and liturgical formation, 131–54; on
mystery of prayer and erroneous forms of prayer, 113–14;
new liturgical movement and
priorities for intervention,
15–17, 91, 96, 131–54; on participation in the liturgy, 138–
40; on Pseudo-Dionysius's
cosmic and liturgical theology,
22–25, 27; *Sacramentum caritatis*,
54, 91, 96, 134–42. See also
*motu proprio Summorum pontifi-
cum* (Benedict XVI's papal
action); Ratzinger, Joseph
Benedictine Rule, 82, 92
Benson, Robert Hugh, 128
Bianchi, Lorenzo, 90n

155